The Silver Lining of Alzheimer's

One Son's Journey Into The Mystery

Eliezer Sobel

Copyright © 2025 Eliezer Sobel

All rights reserved.

This book or parts thereof may not be reproduced in any form or by any means, including electronic, mechanical, photocopying, recording, or otherwise, without the prior written permission of the copyright owner.

www.eliezersobel.com

www.elemipress.com

Published by
ELEMI PRESS
92 Linden Ave
Red Bank, N.J. 07701
FIRST EDITION

Cover Design by: Miblart
Interior Design by Angelee van Allman
Graphic Images: EmbodyArt by Colormaiden
"Tiny Little Bird" photo, Page 91, by Morton Rich
Photographic Assistance: Jay A. Hightman
Elemi Press Website Design: John Rhea

ISBN 978-0997121735
Library of Congress Control Number: 2023914972
Printed in the United States of America

ALSO BY ELIEZER SOBEL

Manual of Good Luck

Wild Heart Dancing: A Personal One-Day Quest To Liberate the Artist & Lover Within

Minyan: Ten Jewish Men in a World That is Heartbroken

The 99th Monkey: A Spiritual Journalist's Misadventures With Gurus, Messiahs, Sex, Psychedelics And Other Consciousness-Raising Experiments

Blue Sky, White Clouds: A Book for Memory-Challenged Adults

L'Chaim! Pictures to Evoke Memories of Jewish Life

Dark Light of the Soul/Encounters with Gabrielle Roth

Mordecai's Book

E-BOOK: *Why I Am Not Enlightened*

DEDICATION

To my beloved parents:

Manya Sobel
January 22, 1924-November 29, 2019

Max Sobel
December 23, 1923-November 11, 2016

My older brother:
Harry Sobel,
who remained my loyal and steadfast
support system throughout the entire affair.

And especially my wife:
Shari Cordon,
who dropped her entire life
to devote herself
full-time to helping care
for my parents for six years.

In memory of my dear, beloved niece,
Amy Elizabeth Sobel

who left us far too soon:
July 13, 1984 – June 30, 2021

See amysobelfoundation.org

CONTENTS

INTRODUCTION
1

ONE
Mom Is Always Right!
7

TWO
Connection
13

THREE
The Happiness of Memory Loss
21

FOUR
Hospital Horrors
27

FIVE
Almost a Doctor
43

SIX
Manya's Story
49

SEVEN
Uncle Norbert
59

EIGHT
The End of Personal History
69

NINE
Life & Death
73

TEN
Word Salad
87

ELEVEN
Mom's Last Vacation
95

TWELVE
Dad's Downfall
101

THIRTEEN
Becoming My Father
109

FOURTEEN
"Better Times Are Coming"
123

FIFTEEN
Shari's Mom
135

SIXTEEN
Dad & Mom's Farewell Scenes
145

EPILOGUE
153

AFTERWORD
157

ACKNOWLEDGMENTS
161

INTRODUCTION

My mother, Manya Sobel, passed from this world in 2019 at the age of ninety-five, after a grueling twenty-year journey into the utter oblivion of Alzheimer's disease. We were very fortunate—or some might say crazy—to be able to care for her at home the entire time. My father, Max, was her sole hands-on caregiver for the first eight years until he finally surrendered to my brother Harry's and my pleading that he allow a home health aide to begin helping him. Even then, for a full year he only permitted someone to come for two hours each morning to help get Mom bathed and dressed for the day.

Soon, however, his aide needed an aide, because it required two people to prep my mother: one to gently restrain her while the other cleaned her up and put her clothes on. Without a second person, Mom would resist the process by pulling the aide's hair, grabbing and tugging at her earrings with great force, and punching and kicking. Harry and I had had to listen through the bathroom door as my Dad attempted to do this on his own for way too long before he finally recognized it was just too much for him.

My father was a World War II veteran who fought in the Battle of the Bulge and came home with a Purple Heart. Like many men of his generation, Max was an incredibly stubborn man in certain areas. Despite being a brilliant and nationally celebrated professor—and every student's *favorite teacher ever*—as well as the author of over sixty mathematics textbooks, he nevertheless had a huge blind spot in regard to my mother's disease.

Ironically, one of his professional specialties was "Teaching Math to the Slow Learner," and yet when it came to being a caregiver for an Alzheimer's patient, he himself proved to be an extremely slow learner. Although he obviously knew what was happening to our mom, he was somehow in great denial at the same time.

One of the more glaring examples of this was that over time my mother grew incontinent—not an uncommon turn of events—but rather than facing the idea of his wife wearing adult undergarments, he persisted for several *years* in allowing her to have "accidents" in public, and developed the habit of bringing along a change of underwear, pants, and baby wipes every time they left the house. Even in restaurants, Dad preferred the struggle of changing Mom in a tiny restroom stall to letting her wear the appropriate protective gear. It was a bit maddening to behold, and very difficult for Harry and me to observe this behavior, but as smart as our father was, we were unable to pierce his resistance in this area.

In retrospect, it is more understandable: when he pre-deceased my mother by three years in 2016, at the age of ninety-two, it was just six weeks shy of what would have been their 70th Anniversary, so it was clearly very difficult for him to accept the fact that his beloved partner of so many years was vanishing before his eyes, and each new step in the process (such as purchasing "Depends," an adult diaper product) must have felt like yet another stab to his heart. Ironically, had he lasted until their seventieth, neither of them would have been aware of the event.

All this to say, despite the positive slant that the title of this book indicates, our family's journey with Mom—and Dad—was no walk in the park. We had the "luxury" of her lasting two decades with Alzheimer's, which enabled us to witness all the stages along the way that most families in a similar situation will immediately recognize. But there are countless books, articles, videos, blogs and social media groups that have amply covered that heart-breaking territory again and again. My intention here is to shine a light on a more positive view on what is ordinarily experienced as "all bad."

It should be said, however, that unlike many families, we were privileged to have the financial means to care for my mother at home for the duration of her illness, and were likewise fortunate to find a physician who provided her with medication that successfully calmed her more explosive and violent periods of anger without unduly sedating her. Both of those factors contributed to avoiding having her wind up being yet another old lady with dementia slumped over in a wheelchair, which is heartbreaking to observe in any visit to a nursing home memory unit.

Please understand that this book is definitely not an attempt to sugarcoat or whitewash the tragic and impossibly difficult aspects of dealing with a family member stricken by Alzheimer's or other forms of dementia; rather, I, the younger son (seventy-two as I write this), am choosing to share the extraordinary blessings and healing moments of laughter and joy that our family *also* experienced with Mom over the years, in order to provide some balance and perhaps even a bit of hope and possibility to others going through a similar ordeal. From my perspective, there was a "glass half-full" version of the story alongside what most people would likely consider to be a glass not half, but completely empty. My focus attempts to balance the all-too-familiar horrors of the illness by also revealing the positive aspects our family experienced: surprising moments of joy, laughter, and healing that emerged, providing us, at times, indeed, with a silver lining of unexpected delight.

For most of my life, whenever I had to fill out an official document, I listed my occupation as "Writer and Teacher." Several years into managing my parents' care, however, upon encountering that blank space on a legal form, without even thinking about it, I simply answered that my occupation was "Caregiver." Then it occurred to me that the next time I came across that question, my response would be honed even further, to merely, "Son."

Hence this disclaimer:

I am not a physician, nurse, social worker or medical professional of any sort. My qualifications for writing this tale are quite simply this:

I am a son, no more, no less.

Eliezer's 40th birthday with his parents, 32 years ago.

©EmbodyArt by Colormaiden

EVER FEEL TRAPPED BY TECHNOLOGY?

For several years—one of Mom's many plateaus and stages—I would SKYPE with both her and Dad every day from our home in Virginia. It was a tricky dance, because Dad was clearly starved for adult, sane conversation, and needed to share every detail of his life with me, while I was wanting to tune in more to my mom and hopefully help to keep me in her consciousness and memory for as long as possible. I would frequently interrupt Dad's daily report by asking Mom a question, to bring her into the conversation.

Invariably she would begin with the same routine every day. Once I got her attention, she would stare at my face on the computer screen with an expression of utter perplexity, and then finally would ask me perhaps one of the all-time greatest questions:

"How long are they going to keep you there, inside that tiny box?"

"Not long, Ma, just until I'm finished talking with you."

"Are they feeding you in there?"

"Yes. I'm fine, they give me plenty to eat."

"Wait, let me get you a glass of water," and she'd stand up and leave the room, returning shortly, water in hand, and start to bring the glass toward my screen image, get momentarily confused, and then would say,

"I'll just set it here for you," and she'd put it on the computer table so I could reach it as needed, through the screen.

Chapter One

Mom is Always Right!

One beautiful autumn afternoon about twenty-three years ago, my wife Shari Cordon and I spent a pleasant hour with my mother, Manya, strolling in a local park, then sharing a wooden bench and gazing together at an elegant and striking, large white egret floating in peaceful stillness on the pond before us. Mom was a youthful seventy-six or so. When we returned home, she approached me only minutes later, with wonderment in her eyes, and asked,

"Did I tell you I saw an egret today?"

I hadn't yet learned the appropriate way to respond to people with memory loss, which would have been to be simply intrigued and join in her wonder by saying,

"No, you didn't, please tell me about it."

Instead, I made the classic mistake of reminding her of "reality"—meaning, *my* reality: the fact that Shari and I had been with her, sitting next to her on the bench where we all saw the egret. I tried to remind her of our walk in the park and our time there together only fifteen minutes earlier. This was clearly the wrong approach, I realized too late, for I was provoking anxiety within her right before my eyes; she was still aware enough to recognize that something was "off," but was not aware enough to be able or willing to acknowledge something was wrong, to either herself or us, much less speak about it.

I had broken Fundamental Principle #1, endlessly repeated by all the experts in caregiving for dementia patients:

Never try to talk someone out of their experience.
Or, put another way:
Never argue with or contradict their reality; always flow with it.

If your loved one says it is Saturday night on a Monday morning, it *is* Saturday night, for *them*. That is what's real for them in that moment, and it is every bit as real to them as your experience that it is "really" Monday morning. If my mother insisted, as she did once, that she had no sister, and never had a sister, just five minutes after speaking with her sister, then, in that moment, in her experience of reality, she truly had no sister. Period.

Think about it: to her quite reasonable way of thinking, surely if she had a sister, she of all people would obviously know about it. Only a crazy person would dispute that simple fact. My older brother Harry and I patiently tried to explain Principle #1 to our father, after time and again observing his increasing frustration and short fuse with Mom. He would sit and listen to us patiently, nodding his head, seemingly understanding us. Yet only a few minutes later we would again hear him upstairs raising his voice, shouting things like, "OF COURSE YOU HAVE A SISTER! HER NAME IS GERDA! YOU JUST GOT OFF THE PHONE WITH HER!"

After one such incident, my mother grabbed my elbow and took me aside privately, quietly saying, "I think there's something's wrong with your father; he's been acting very strange lately." I couldn't help but burst out laughing, because I got it. For a moment, I saw how the world looked through my mother's eyes. In her *"I have no sister"* world, my father appeared like an out-of-control, screaming lunatic, asserting a fictitious *"you* do *have a sister"* reality. It reminded me of those cartoons of people speaking to their cat, and all the cat hears are random incomprehensible sounds. So yes, through her eyes, Dad was the crazy one. Which I found simultaneously hilarious and deeply sad, and Harry and I continued to do our best to coach our poor father in the art of being with Mom in a way that would allow both of them more peace.

Manya (right) with her sister Gerda

After a particularly tough visit home, witnessing a lot of conflict between my parents, before departing, I left a note on Dad's desk, in big letters:

REMEMBER:
No matter what she says,
Mom is ALWAYS RIGHT...
ABOUT EVERYTHING!!!

Easier said than done when you have been married for over sixty years, as countless kneejerk reactions and automatic behaviors grow deeply and habitually embedded in the groove of how you have always been together. Again, the way of interacting suggested by Principle #1 is to simply affirm and always agree with the person's version of reality, never to argue with it or correct it. It is difficult at first, but it is an invaluable skill that I found is quite possible to learn.

For example, Mom often uttered what is a common refrain heard from Alzheimer's patients: "I want to go home," even though she was already at home. Rather than try to persuade her of the error in her thinking, as my dad would be inclined to do—"YOU *ARE* HOME!"—I would demonstrate an alternative response. "Okay, Mom," I'd say, "I'll take you home," and I'd take her by the hand and walk her out of whatever room we were in, and by the time we got to, say, the hallway, her attention would be drawn to an old family photo on the wall and she would stop to study it and talk to me about each of the people in the picture, and forget all about our purported journey back home. This is sometimes referred to in the field as "redirecting." That is also one of the chief benefits of the Alzheimer's patient being "in the moment;" when there's a bad moment, it can change immediately if the person is skillfully redirected, much like a baby can go from screaming bloody murder to happily smiling in the blink of an eye.

"Home Sweet Home." It is a useful self-inquiry to imagine exactly what that word "home" means to a person, for we all share that primordial longing for a familiar and cozy place of utter safety, warmth and comfort. Such a desire harkens back, if not to the womb, then perhaps to a memory; for me, I'd be three or four years old, happy and relaxed, feeling loved, both of my parents at home, and all of us together, peaceful, and above all *safe*.

Robert Frost wrote, "Home is the place where, when you have to go there, they have to take you in." And Maurice Sendak ended his famed book, *Where the Wild Things Are*, with

> "And [he] sailed back over a year
> and in and out of weeks and through a day
> and into the night of his very own room
> where he found his supper waiting for him
> and it was still hot."

Thus, "Home is the place they have to take you in," where "supper is waiting and still hot." We all long to get back to such a home whenever we feel ourselves alone, abandoned, frightened and alienated in this big, wide, world, like a lost child in a massive, teeming crowd, panicking, desperately searching for that elusive place where all safety lies. Obviously, then, what a person needs in such a situation is compassionate, comforting care, not correction, criticism or contradiction.

To my eyes, my mother was actually becoming more and more like a delightful and innocent child, yet Dad was desperately still clinging to his long-held idea of her as the person she used to be, and he kept trying to make her conform to that picture despite the growing evidence to the contrary.

Mom is always right about everything.

When skillfully applied, this simple shift in perspective changes the whole picture. Mostly what it changes is inevitable conflict and upsetting encounters, and instead allows for what can often be a fascinating glimpse into another's inner universe. It is actually not very different than playing with a child whose active imagination creates fantasy worlds all the time. If you were baby-sitting a four-year-old who told you she was a princess living on the moon, would you try to explain to her that the moon can't support life, and unless she was born into or marries into royalty, she has no shot at being a princess? (The answer is obvious, unless you're *really bad* at babysitting!) But my father didn't quite grasp that it often appeared to us as if he was arguing with a toddler about the nature of reality.

One evening, early on, Mom got lost driving home from the local shopping mall, five minutes from my parents' house. She had been going to that mall at least two or three times a week for some fifty years. When I very gently suggested to her that something didn't sound right, and that perhaps we should get her checked out by a doctor, she angrily snapped at me:

"YOU WOULD HAVE GOTTEN LOST TOO, IT WAS VERY DARK OUT."

End of discussion. In that instant I saw that she would likely never be open to a frank and honest conversation about what was happening to her. And I also saw that it wasn't my place, or anyone's place, to force her to do it.

(By the way, just so you know, this is not a book about "principles," so just because I described Principle #1, please don't be waiting around for #2; there isn't one, at least not in this book.)

MOMENTS WITH MANYA

Mom thought she noticed some sort of funny look on my face one day, and asked,

"What's the matter?"

"Life," I answered.

"Oh," she said, "I had that yesterday."

Chapter Two

Connection

In the first years of my mother's disease, my friends would often approach me with a forlorn, fearful look on their faces, and very hesitantly ask, "Does she still know who you are?" as if that were the single, most important factor, and if my answer was "No, she doesn't," there was absolutely nothing worse they could possibly imagine. They found the very idea to be horrifying.

I, on the other hand, would inwardly respond with the thought, "*I* don't really know who I am; why would I care if *she* does?" For I had discovered something much deeper and far more important to me than whether my mother still knew who I was or understood how we were related: very simply, it was *connection,* on a deep, soul-to-soul level, beyond language and memory.

As my mother's cognitive abilities slowly slipped away, I gradually recognized that the love and connection between us remained unwavering—at least for the first fifteen years or so—and in fact, our love seemed to be deepening, growing and expressing itself in ways it never did before she got the disease. I was stunned when I suddenly realized one day that Alzheimer's was actually healing our relationship.

It was the exact opposite of what most people fear. Whether or not my mother knew my name or knew that I was her son, if we could still love and laugh together, and feel our connection, the rest truly became utterly irrelevant to me. If you get nothing else from this book, please understand this:

Connection is everything.

I actually found myself being grateful to Alzheimer's, for in a very strange way, it was giving my mother back to me, when all the outward evidence pointed in the other direction. To all appearances, it sure seemed that she was being taken away from us, and that is undoubtedly how most families experience the journey of dementia in a spouse or parent. I'm certain that my father, understandably, experienced it that way.

But that just wasn't the case for me. My mother's process with Alzheimer's provided an unexpected opportunity to open my heart and heal old wounds. I could finally feel, and openly express, as well as receive, the underlying love between us that had been covered over and withheld for so many years beneath a difficult history of anger, hurt, and mutual misunderstanding. Despite the assistance of at least a dozen therapists and countless alternative self-help explorations over the years, for much of my adult life I had inwardly remained a resentful, closed-up, and unforgiving teenager in relationship to both of my parents.

Yet the quality and level of relationship and loving connection with my mother, which I had been longing for and struggling to achieve my entire adult life, actually came to pass effortlessly once she had Alzheimer's. But that could never have happened if I had made it about *me*, and whether or not she knew me or remembered our shared life together, or remembered anything at all, for that matter. I saw her instead with new eyes, and discovered the person that was still right there—right *here*—still responding in a very real way.

Connect to the actual person who is here now,
not the person you remember and wish they still were.

We did whatever it took to make that connection. It might have been listening to music together; dancing; looking at a picture book or photo album for the fortieth time; singing old familiar songs or humming without any words; or just silently holding hands, offering tender caresses or a foot rub. There most definitely was a human being inside there that felt and responded to love and touch and registered it on a cellular level, just as a baby responds to love and touch without the benefit of language. I couldn't help but conclude—and feel—that our two souls were truly communing regardless of the missing verbal and mental elements of normal communication and the absence of shared history and language.

We sat at a piano together once and she selected a note and played it repeatedly—in perfect 4/4 time—and I improvised over her tone. She kept perfect rhythm, and we enjoyed a shared moment of co-creation that delighted both of us.

Going further back in time, when she was more present and still communicating verbally, one day my father was complaining about how difficult it was to find things to do with Mom apart from parking her in front of the TV. I tried to demonstrate for Dad how easy it was to find activities to do with her. I took a box of coins from his office to the kitchen, poured them on the table, and proceeded to spend at least an hour with my mother, playing a dozen different games, including: separate the shiny pennies from the old faded ones; stack the nickels; create a face on the table with the dimes; put the quarters back in the box; move everything around randomly for no reason; on and on. We never ran out of things to do. I said to my father, "And the best part of it, Dad, is that you can put the coins away and bring them out tomorrow and do the whole thing over again, and she won't remember ever having done it before."

I went home, and the next night I got a call from Dad. I asked him if he had tried playing the coin games with Mom.

"Yeah but it didn't work," he said dejectedly, "she couldn't tell a nickel from a dime."

I was flabbergasted that he could so totally miss the point. His years of linear mathematical processing wouldn't let him think outside the box and enter the improvised world of pure play.

Similarly, one afternoon my niece Julie, my mother, and I sat down at the dining room table with a deck of cards. I dealt each of us five cards, and there was a tangerine on the table. Mom studied her hand intently. Nobody, mind you, had uttered a word about what game we were playing. Julie went first and put down a ten of clubs, moved the tangerine next to the saltshaker, and selected a new card, all of us giggling. I picked up her ten, discarded a King of Hearts and Three of Clubs as a pair, representing some unknown, mysterious alliance, and placed the tangerine on top of them. Our giggling evolved to contained hilarity.

Mom studied her cards, furrowed her brow, looked down at the table, back at her hand, then back at the table again. She finally discarded a Four of Spades, reached for the tangerine, began peeling and eating it, all of us now laughing hysterically. The game went on for at least thirty minutes, as my father stood by, watching and befuddled, trying to grasp the rules and asking someone to teach him how to play. I said,

"Well...that's the easy part, Dad: there *are* no rules!" But it left him baffled.

It occurs to me that I may seem to be painting a portrait of my father as if he were some sort of clueless buffoon, but there could be nothing further from the truth. My dad, Dr. Max A. Sobel, as I've said, was a highly distinguished, revered, and well-known mathematics professor around the country and was known as a "Teacher's Teacher," respected and loved far and wide within the mathematics education field, commanding standing-room-only crowds at his lectures, which were frequently peppered with magic tricks and brilliant humor. He taught into his early 80s, and would frequently receive random fan letters from students he had instructed half a century earlier who had never forgotten him, thanking him for changing their lives forever.

He finally retired to stay home and care for Mom. Even at 90, he was computer literate and we communicated daily via email and SKYPE, and he was managing a very complex household, driving and shopping, paying the bills, supervising lawn and house maintenance, and doing all the cooking. (Although I *did* have to coach him about how to cook eggs and put a piece of salmon in the oven.) However, I *did* wonder if it was time to worry when he started doing things like leaving the burner on the stove lit for seven hours. (I worried even more when it occurred to me that I was home at the time.) Or putting a plastic container in the oven, creating a mac and cheese—and plastic—that was a lot more gooey than usual.

After finally agreeing to the first home health aide in the house, eventually, with our help, he went on to hire and schedule seven more aides on a piecemeal, hourly schedule, using a highly complicated system of recordkeeping. My father, as everyone who knew him would attest, was quite competent, despite my mother's frequent assessment that, "Max can't hammer a nail in straight." In fact, all those who saw what he was doing for Mom in order to keep her comfortably at home considered him to be nothing less than a saint.

I tell the stories about the coins and what we came to refer to as "Tangerine Poker" in order to indicate how difficult it can be for even the smartest and most educated people to adjust to the transformation of a spouse who has memory loss, after years and years of habitual ways of relating and being.

I also tell the stories to suggest that all caregivers would be well-served by loosening up their rational left brains a bit and allowing the right brain of intuition, spontaneity and creative play to emerge more, if possible. For that is the entrée point into your loved one's world and reality, and that's where you most want to be: inside their world with them. That's where you'll find the connection you may have thought you were losing. Our sense of connection is far deeper than the recollections of shared time together that are disappearing daily, wiping out the history of our relationship.

Connection is everything.

MOMENTS WITH MANYA

One day we were sitting at the kitchen table and Mom had a glass of apple juice, and was very closely examining it from all angles, lifting it up to the light, turning it around, tapping it gently with a fork in several places, causing different "ping" sounds. Finally, it appeared that her research was complete. She put the glass and the fork down, looked up at us, and remarked,

"I wonder what size brassiere it wears?"

©EmbodyArt by Colormaiden

WATCHING HER DIET

Overnight, Mom went from being fanatically concerned with her fat and cholesterol intake, for years eating only egg-white omelets and low-fat everything, to suddenly *only* eating the yellow yolks and throwing the egg whites away, as well as eating chocolate, potato chips and ice cream all day—unheard of in our house—making up for lost time.

Chapter Three

The Happiness of Memory Loss

When Mom first started showing signs of Mild Cognitive Impairment (MCI), I had a session with a psychic. I told her I was worried about my mother losing her memory. The psychic paused a moment, looked inward for a message or response, then said,

"I think your mother is going to be a lot happier *without* her memories."

And wow, did she nail that one.

As her memories faded and her cognitive abilities receded—the horrific aspects notwithstanding—my mother became increasingly funny and free and began to shine with an inner and outer beauty, radiating love to everyone she met and often laughing uproariously multiple times a day, usually for no reason at all. As a result, the transformation of my relationship with Mom just happened by itself, for I would have had to be an unthinkably hard-hearted person to remain stuck in a childish, unforgiving place in the presence of the radiant being my mother had magically become.

It made sense that my mother would be happier without her memories, for she was haunted throughout her life by what she witnessed as a young teenager in Nazi Germany, before escaping with her family to America. As one of the only Jewish kids in her one-room German schoolhouse, the Nazi teacher made her stand in front of the class and read aloud from the rabidly antisemitic tabloid,

Der Sturmer, which referred to Jews as "vermin," and described how to properly recognize a Jew, accompanied by diagrams of their noses and skulls. Some of her classmates—Fritz was the name she mentioned—would become or were already part of Hitler Youth. When her teacher asked her a question, if she didn't answer quickly enough, he smacked her hands forcefully with a wooden ruler.

In my childhood, whenever there was any visual image on TV that depicted Hitler or goose-stepping German soldiers adorned with swastikas, my mother would visibly panic, as if she were having a bad LSD flashback, and my father would quickly jump up and change the channel. I was very young and had no idea what any of that was about. But there was something very bad, ominous and unspoken about whatever it was. It left my mother very frightened in the world, hiding behind a congenial social veneer. Her fundamental trust in others—any people other than Jews, and ultimately, anyone other than her immediate family—was damaged forever. She lived in an us/them world, while my life was more and more focused on breaking that barrier down. This different way of perceiving reality was an endless source of conflict between us.

Many years later, I attended a ten-day "Bearing Witness" retreat at Auschwitz with the Zen Peacemaker's Order. The few hundred of us spent each day at the camp in the freezing cold of Poland's winter, clutching the single soup bowl we had been given for the experience, and each evening we would meet in small groups to share. Only about twenty percent of the retreat participants were Jewish, and in our small sharing group there were several people like me—children of survivors—as well as several children of SS officers.

We discovered something very fascinating together. Both the Jewish descendants of Holocaust survivors, as well as the offspring of Nazi officers, had experienced an identical dynamic regarding the atrocities of World War II in our childhood homes growing up:

Utter silence.

Whether we were little Jewish kids living in America or little German children being raised in "the Fatherland," we all recollected an identical, eerie silence in our households around a particular, unnamed subject that we wouldn't recognize as the Holocaust until many years later, as adults. Only odd looks between our parents punctuated the silence.

But as her memories of the Holocaust began to fade, the beautiful innocent girl my mother was before being traumatized began to reemerge, like a flower coming back to life after a long winter. I knew the process was complete one day as I was helping her on with her jacket. As she stuck her arm through the sleeve, she inadvertently wound up with her arm raised in the Seig Heil position, and spontaneously said aloud, "Heil Hitler" and cracked up laughing. She would never—*ever*—have even uttered that name, let alone said those words and laughed.

The psychic had definitely been right: Mom was happier without her memories.

And so was I.

I once informed my mother as she lay on a hospital gurney that she was about to have an endoscopy, and she thought it was the funniest thing she'd ever heard. She was laughing uproariously as they wheeled her away. She had become exquisitely innocent, happy and childlike, filled with an infectious joy and wonder, qualities reflecting the essence of who she truly was that I had been unable to see previously. (Of course, she did an amazing job at hiding those qualities behind a critical and often explosive German-Jewish persona, filled with fear, rage and deep sorrow.)

MOMENTS WITH MANYA

Once, out of the blue, she announced:
"I'm such a nice person and I can't help it."

~~~~~

As I was leaving the house one afternoon, she spontaneously came out with,
"If anything goes wrong, call 911."

©EmbodyArt by Colormaiden

THE CASE OF THE MISSING BRISKET

I joined my parents to run some errands, including a visit to the kosher butcher to buy a piece of brisket for an upcoming holiday. We returned home, and the brisket was nowhere to be found. We searched the car and the house, and then retraced our steps in our minds and called the various places we had been, starting with the butcher, thinking maybe we had left it at the cashier's station. No such luck. We called the post office and the bakery. Nobody had spotted the elusive slab of raw meat anywhere. Purely by accident, Dad opened Mom's pocketbook which she still carried around when they went out, but which was always completely empty. *Usually*. On this particular day, it made for a cozy, one-room enclosed space for, you guessed it, the mysterious runaway brisket.

Chapter Four

Hospital Horrors

It is quite common for people with Alzheimer's disease to become extremely agitated, angry, defiant, even violent at times. My mother went through a stage when we had to hide all the knives in the house, because she had taken to chasing aides around, brandishing a meat cleaver. She sometimes threw heavy objects in a rage, ripped up precious, ancient photos, and would scream at her own image in the mirror. I sometimes felt like I was in a sequel to *The Exorcist,* as she often truly sounded like she was channeling Satan.

As a result, for a time she became completely impossible to manage at home and we had to reluctantly admit her to a psychiatric lockdown unit in a hospital for ten days, which was a total nightmare. She first had to go through a torturous seven-hour admission procedure in the ER, for which a urine sample was required, and that impossible feat could only be accomplished by five people holding her down and another inserting a catheter, a scene only Harry observed, and said he would never forget, nor ever tell us about in further detail. One would think that for an Alzheimer's patient in her eighties being admitted to a psychiatric unit, the medical personnel would recognize that perhaps they could get by without a urine sample. But no.

Although my mother—and later, my father—were only ever in upscale, highly-rated, New Jersey hospitals in the New York metropolitan area, as we noticed more and more errors and oversights in their care over time, it was a stunning revelation to finally recognize that *we* were actually in charge of her care in those facilities. It was also painfully obvious that most people don't know this, and simply assume that everything the doctors say and do is correct, and most patients and their families are simply trusting, intimidated and obedient. They have obviously not seen one of the scariest statistics I've ever come across, that originated in a 2016 study at Johns Hopkins University:

"Medical Errors are the 3rd Leading Cause of Death in the U.S."

We quickly figured out that one of us needed to be in the psych ward at all times to advocate for my mother, and it was truly sad to see other patients, seemingly abandoned, who never appeared to have any visitors at all. The need for our presence hit home one day when we came in and glanced at the daily nursing board, where it clearly stated, "Today's nurse for Manya Sobel is: Jackie." Yet we were there from eight am until Mom's bedtime at nine pm, and we never even met this mysterious Jackie. We also quickly figured out that it was apparently up to *us* to remind the staff when it was time for Mom's medicines as well as which ones, and also when she needed to be changed or have her bed cleaned.

At home, my father had developed all sorts of skillful tricks to get Mom to take various medications; they all involved crushing the pills and mixing the result into sweets of one kind or another. It kept getting harder to fool her, and his methods had progressed from sprinkling the pulverized meds on the crumb topping of a raspberry tart, to hiding them inside a chocolate wafer cookie, the preparation of which required virtually a surgeon's skill and precision, to concealing them within a scoop of vanilla ice cream dripping with Hershey's fudge sauce, covered with a liberal topping of whipped cream. In other words, my mother required an ice cream sundae just to take a single pill.

In the psych ward, my father tried to explain to mean Nurse Ratched (to be fair, most nurses we encountered had hearts of gold) that her approach of trying to force Mom to swallow a pill would be unsuccessful, but his plea fell on deaf ears. She insisted she'd have no problem and we watched in horror as she again and again attempted to literally shove a spoonful of applesauce containing a pill through my mother's clenched teeth, most of it winding up on the floor while my Mom was yelling and punching her. Ratched finally surrendered, and it was with some measure of vindication that I observed her watching Dad prepare his special sundae concoction he had brought from home, and easily feed it to Mom, a minor victory over the system.

Even with us there to advocate, we couldn't protect my mother from the callous indifference of some of the hospital practices. She had stopped using the shower and bath years earlier after she was unable to lift herself out of the tub one time and panicked, and she remained terrified of immersing herself in water for the rest of her life. As a result, our home aides had become experts at administrating in-bed sponge baths, including hair-washing. Yet in the hospital we had to stand idly by as no less than three men grabbed her and carried her into the shower room, removed her gown and literally hosed her down as she screamed bloody murder. She emerged afterward and fell into my arms, weeping. I'm certain that in her experience it must have felt like she was in a concentration camp in the hands of Nazis.

At one point I had to loudly threaten to remove her from the hospital "Against Medical Advice" when I overheard that they intended to restrain her while administering various tests for symptoms of stomach problems she never had. Someone had inaccurately reported multiple episodes of vomiting that simply were not the case. Restraining an Alzheimer's patient is never a good idea, and I knew that the experience would further traumatize her.

Miraculously, after ten days, the doctors were able to find the right dosage of a medication that worked to calm Mom's violent behaviors without overly sedating her, and she never again went through another violent period, nor did she need the medication forever. The blessing of Alzheimer's was that her memory of that place and what she went through there vanished as soon as we got her out.

I'm well aware that not all families are as lucky as we were, to find a magic pill that "fixes" the most difficult aspects of the disease. In the personal stories of Alzheimer's that millions of families around the world can tell, there are no two exactly alike. You may or may not be able to even relate to my perspective, or my version of how things unfolded for us and my mother—and later, my father; and later still, my mother-in-law—but my desire is that our family's story will convey at least a glimmer of possibility and hope that perhaps all is not quite as black and white or as purely horrific and tragic as it may often seem. We discovered along the way that there really *can* be hidden joys on the road to oblivion; I experienced new expressions of love and levels of connection with my mother that I never expected; we often shared spontaneous laughter and hilarity, as well as many poignant and tender moments of a new and different sort of intimacy that was not rooted in linear understanding or making any sense verbally, but were nevertheless very precious, bittersweet gifts of the heart.

So it may not be all bad news, contrary to what we may have thought and felt at the beginning. But to locate the positive aspects in our journey with Mom, we all had to learn to look with new eyes and be willing to relinquish our deeply ingrained viewpoints, allowing for a uniquely different way of seeing the situation. Over time, our family had to reframe what often seemed to be nothing less than one of the most awful fates for any person or family to witness and endure. In so doing, we discovered there was another way of being with what initially appeared to be a catastrophic turn of events; a new and different way of seeing and responding to the seeming horror story that was occurring in our family. There was an alternate view of things that we were able to slowly cultivate, one which actually revealed positive and life-affirming aspects of the tale that we had been overlooking.

My experience taught me that there is a hidden dimension to this most unusual of journeys, one that is not often spoken of or usually even noticed or experienced, but which is nevertheless possible, present and available for those of us who are willing to see it, open to it, and embrace the *Silver Lining of Alzheimer's*.

It's highly unlikely that there are many of us who can make this leap in our perception of what appears to be a terrible and irreparable turn of events in the life of a loved one, and in our own lives. It is certainly impossible to come to a more positive outlook without first enduring the heart-dropping and agonizing realization that one of the most dearly cherished and beloved human beings in our lives—whether it be a spouse, parent, sibling, or close friend—is slowly "losing it."

What exactly is the "it" they are beginning to lose? Nothing short of their very identity, as defined by their own, and everyone else's, memories of all they have been, all that they have done with us, without us, and with others, the sum total of the myriad and endless factors that have hitherto coalesced into the very personhood of who they are and have always been, both to themselves and to us and to all their loved ones.

In a way it can feel like a fate worse than death, for when someone actually dies, whether slowly through disease or old age, or quickly through a sudden event like a car accident or worse, despite the great suffering of loss and grief it will trigger in us, it is nevertheless unambiguous: Our beloved is clearly gone. We have viewed them in a casket being lowered into the ground or placed into a crematorium and taken their ashes home with us. We have witnessed their lifeless body up close, and know deep within, beneath our immediate emotional trauma or even denial at first, that they are absolutely no longer with us in the land of the living. The grief may be unbearable at times, but there is definitely closure.

Why is Alzheimer's possibly a "fate worse than death"? Precisely because all the elements of actual physical death are absent. At ninety-five, shortly before she finally passed, my mother continued to have perfect vital signs according to her visiting doctor and was on virtually no medications as many elderly folks are. For the first years of the disease, we still see the person's familiar body moving, breathing, eating, speaking (making less and less sense over time), and at least initially, continuing to exhibit all the activities and signs of life shared by the rest of us, albeit with increasing quirks.

But something far deeper and more essential is gradually fading from view: Their very persona, comprised of the history and life events they have lived through, is somehow getting "blurry." A sort of amnesia appears to be taking root. Their relationship to ordinary reality that everyone else takes for granted is shifting, and that is no minor thing. Although it starts out small, with little incidents of forgetfulness, it gradually progresses and eventually falls further and further down a dark tunnel into a completely alternative reality that the rest of us can't begin to imagine or understand.

But what we can and must do, as a good place to start, is to recognize and acknowledge the existence of their new and strange reality and affirm that it is as valid a way to subjectively view the world as our own.

We can't argue with someone's direct, personal experience.

If, for example, you were to tell me that you felt cold, and my response was, "No, you are not feeling cold," I will cause an instant and unnecessary conflict between us. For the only authority about what we are experiencing is ourselves. The Alzheimer's or dementia patient is the absolute authority about what they think, believe and experience, and our only job is to "get it," not to change it, fix it, or convince them otherwise. It is called "compassionate listening," a receiving of someone's experience with no personal agenda to have it be any different than it is.

(Ironically, this is the identical attitude that is applicable to *all* of our relationships.)

When we misplace our keys or enter a room and forget why we went in there, such events are usually referred to as "senior moments," not all that worrisome, and quite common. My friend Randy told me he once gathered his laundry and brought it out to his car to take to the laundromat. Alas, he pulled into the parking lot of the post office, grabbed his dirty clothes, walked into the building, and only then did he look around and recognize his error. "I realized I only had two choices," he told me. "I could either mail my laundry to myself, or sheepishly slink out of the building." A vital distinction is made, however, between such episodes of distraction, and when someone doesn't merely misplace their keys, but in fact, no longer knows what keys *are*. That is a life-shattering difference. Forgetting that we left our shoes in the garage before entering the house is light years away from discovering a family member's Nikes in the freezer.

As more and more such incidents occur, we are eventually forced to reckon with the fact that our loved one's "senior moments" are no trivial matter to be casually dismissed, but rather, are increasingly signs of a serious cognitive disorder that can and only will get worse. We have no choice but to confront head-on a difficult realization: Our loved one is slowly approaching a mysterious Land of Dementia where we won't be able to follow, one that will eventually rob them of everything we've always known them to be; and worse, everything they've always known *themselves* to be. And a journey into that abyss is a one-way trip with no turning back, no hope of recovery (thus far), and the shocking recognition that things will only progress in a downward spiral toward the ultimate oblivion of actual personal disappearance.

But the key word there is "personal." Yes, all that was personal about the person is fading from view. Shared memories are disappearing at an alarming rate. Your spouse, say, who has been your partner and confidante for years, has gradually morphed into your patient. He or she has become someone for you to care for, but you have lost your partner in the process, and there is no longer anyone to talk to, certainly not in the idiosyncratic manner that was unique to your marriage. No one truly knows you the way they did, and that precious part is gone forever. It takes the popular expression "Don't take it personally" to a whole new level.

But what of the *impersonal*? Try to pay attention to the fact that while all that is familiar appears to be exiting stage right, all that is new and unknown is quietly entering from the left. If you have ever been alone in a beautiful place in nature—on the beach at sunset, atop a mountain ridge, or beneath a magical waterfall in a hidden glen—you may have experienced a blissful connection to the impersonal. You probably know nothing at all about the trees surrounding you; many of us don't even know their names, and certainly nothing about their ancestral history. And yet we can nevertheless feel a full sense of appreciation, awe, and even love for the mere existence of these varied living creatures all around us.

Our loved one with advanced memory loss is just such a creature; they are clearly a conscious and sentient being responding to their environment, and to you, in whatever way they do. To truly see them through those eyes is to behold a being who is as wondrous and mysterious as if we were to come across a snow leopard while climbing Mt. Everest. We'd stop dead in our tracks and gaze in wonder.

Our loved one has become someone as delicate and precious as a small child, innocent again. When we can truly see who they are through that lens, we might even experience a twinge of jealousy: "Oh to be pure and true again, to see life through the eyes of the child I once was, my vision unclouded by years of baggage, my accumulated collection of regrets, resentments, dashed hopes, and abandoned dreams." I watched my mother, who I had only known as someone afraid of most people and living behind a mask, evolve, through the "blessing" of Alzheimer's, into her inner child in such a way as to evoke within me a longing for a similar return to innocence. I watched her interacting with complete strangers as well as close family members (who were rapidly becoming strangers) with an equally embracing, open-hearted spirit and joy I could only aspire to. It eventually dawned on me that she was also seeing *me* as if for the first time, yet always with the unconditional love she seemed to gradually be extending to everyone. (Although her aides always insisted that she responded to me differently than others, that she somehow knew we were more connected and that she somehow felt her deep, motherly love long after she knew my name or even what a "son" is.)

One time the four of us were exiting a restaurant. Harry, Dad, and I were in front with Mom bringing up the rear. When we got outside, however, we suddenly realized Mom was missing; she had not followed us out. We looked through the restaurant's picture window and witnessed something astonishing. Mom, who had always had "stranger-danger," was going from table to table on her way out, striking up conversations with all the other diners. To say that that was out of character would be a huge understatement.

Connection is everything.

Given the grim prognosis that the slow and inexorable progression of the disease is certain, it would be shallow and ridiculous to suggest to those who live with and love someone on this journey to just "accept it" and "see the bright side." Such shallow and useless advice is very much *not* what I mean by the silver lining of Alzheimer's. For what I am speaking of is buried under thick layers of deep emotional loss, grief and shock. In a way, the process caregivers go through is not unlike the well-known "Stages of Death and Dying" popularized by Elizabeth Kübler-Ross in the seventies.

The first stage she spoke of, when confronting the fact of one's own impending death due to terminal illness, is "Denial," and as I've indicated, my poor, loving father demonstrated that stage to the fullest for as long as humanly possible. Likewise, Kübler-Ross's second stage, "Anger," became increasingly evident in the way my father responded to Mom's decline, as he continued to "loudly insist" that her perceptions of reality were simply wrong, as if correcting her with more volume, intensity and anger would somehow snap her out of it and she would inexplicably be instantly restored to the person he expected and knew her to be.

Over the years, Kübler-Ross's neatly packaged progression of stages was largely debunked, in that it became clear that people don't move through them in a logical or linear fashion. Rather, they might suddenly and unexpectedly leap from "Denial" all the way to the final stage of "Acceptance," then just as suddenly find themselves in the "Anger" zone once again. And if there's one thing to be learned about working with the memory-impaired person, it's that they will never conform to a predictable set of rules, stages or expectations, and nor will you or those around them. We need to acclimate to a new set of rules in which Stage One may lead to Stage Four, back to Two, then suddenly land us in some new, unnamed stage that Kübler-Ross never even imagined: Stage 28, say. It might be some previously unreported mental/emotional condition that can't even be described, and sometimes only barely felt, but nevertheless dominates our consciousness and daily perception of life. Yes, the analogy breaks down, but it remains interesting to consider that both the actual death of ourselves or a loved one so accurately mirrors the slow loss of someone to dementia. (I skipped Kübler-Ross's third stage, which she called "Bargaining," because it was not directly analogous to the disease progression, although I can easily imagine that it *could* be for some people: "I'll make you a deal, God: if you restore my wife's brain to normal, I will go to church every Sunday, I promise.")

Caregiving for a loved one with Alzheimer's is more like a game of "Chutes and Ladders" than it is a predictable, linear series of steps we can anticipate and prepare for with any degree of certainty or confidence. Each and every one of us in a caregiving capacity is ultimately just "winging it," figuring things out as we go. We just never know what will happen next. At the risk of offering "TMI"—"Too Much Information"—I vividly recall the day my mother entered my father's office where he was working at his computer, and handed him something wrapped in a napkin, saying, "I don't know where this goes." He took it from her, unwrapped it, and discovered a sample of her own feces. Where was *that* written in any of the caregiving books he had read by that time? And the very next day she had apparently mistaken a ceramic bowl on the dining room table for a toilet. Fortunately, those were both single, isolated incidents.

While there are literally thousands of books on the subject of caregiving for an Alzheimer's patient, there are many millions of actual people and real families out there, each undergoing a unique experience that simply cannot be quantified or perfectly captured in a book. Nevertheless, we all read the books anyway, including this one, or we attend a support group, because we are desperate for guidance and help, and sometimes just one sentence, or one connection with another human in the same situation, is sufficient to gently move us along in the letting-go process. Misery really does love company. It really does help to hear other people's stories and feelings, and to recognize that we are not alone. (Note: Along those lines, there are currently close to 30,000 members of a Facebook group called "Memory People," an excellent source of sharing, compassionate listening, and useful information.)

All this to say, there are many stages a caregiver or loved one needs to move through internally before even remotely having a chance to discover the silver lining within their seeming horror story. Kübler-Ross's fourth stage is "Depression," and I personally believe that that one is less of a stage than it is a *context*, an omnipresent backdrop that is all-pervasive and often clearly present throughout all the other stages.

The last one, "Acceptance," does, in fact, correlate directly to what I am suggesting in dealing with losing a loved one to memory loss. Until and unless we can crawl through all the difficult states of mind and feelings that naturally arise in the presence of such a dramatic loss—particularly Denial, Anger and Depression—we will never reach the far lighter, more easygoing world of Acceptance; and yet, it is only once we are there that the potential discovery of the silver lining can even enter our perceptual field and begin to take root in our innermost being. That is to say, the price of admission to this new way of seeing and experiencing is quite steep.

To reiterate, I am not saying "Cheer up, snap out of it, take it easy, accept your situation and get on with it, look on the bright side." Not at all. As a teacher of mine once insisted, "There's no way out but through." We will all have to go through our own unique progression of stages in our own way, for as long as it takes. We can't force ourselves to feel differently than we feel. Or pretend we don't feel the way we *do* feel. This is one situation where "fake it 'til you make it" does not apply. However, the purpose of this book is to potentially awaken you to another realm of possibility that can open up a whole new world inside of you, if and when you've finally suffered through the intense agony of loss and grief and at last found a degree of acceptance.

It is then, and only then, that like an actual, physical death of someone, we have truly said good-bye to our beloved parent, spouse, sibling or friend; we have let them go, continued to cherish the memories of our shared lives together, but unlike observing a deceased one being covered by six feet of dirt, instead we find ourselves graced by the continued presence of a brand new human being in our lives. Perhaps they will be virtually unrecognizable at first, bearing little to no resemblance to the person we remember, yet they are nevertheless still quite alive and *in our lives*, still able to see, speak, and most of all, relate. (At least in the beginning.) They can and will still respond to touch, like all mammals do; they can and will still interact with us, even if their responses are possibly incomprehensible, nonsensical—or at times, hostile—and reflect an upside-down world that is perfectly natural and logical to them, but unrecognizable to us. And therein lies the possibility of magic, the rare and amazing opportunity to discover the mysteries of a whole new world of experience and perception.

It is the very opposite of "Denial"; instead, it is an "embracing" that results from a deep curiosity and desire to explore and understand a reality we've never been privy to before. It can be a fascinating world to discover, in which up is down, black is white, yesterday is tomorrow, and the sky is green. It can provide the same type of joy as hanging out with an infant or toddler who is continuously wide-eyed with wonder, seeing everything for the first time. The person we are caregiving, once we've fully mourned the loss of their prior identity, can suddenly be experienced, with great surprise, not merely as a constant reminder of tragic loss, but rather, as a gift. We have actually been graced to spend intimate time with a being who is unimpeded by historical baggage, someone who has the capacity of perceiving the world directly, through the innocent eyes of a child.

This is undoubtedly why nursing homes have had such positive results having their patients receive visits from little children. They share a mutual openness to the moment and a deep joy in sharing it.

And that, dear reader, is the silver lining.

"Manya through the looking glass, where black is white,
up is down, yesterday is tomorrow, and the sky is green."

MOMENTS WITH MANYA

I was headed up the stairs.

"Where are you going?" she asked me.

"Upstairs," I said.

"Until Wednesday?" she asked.

~~~~~

The phone rang, and she picked it up. We listened to her tell whoever it was that "Everything's fine. We're all here buying chickens." After she hung up, we asked her who it was, and she explained,

"It was all about pillows and teeth."

We never learned who the caller had been.

©EmbodyArt by Colormaiden

CHANGING THE CHANNEL?

Mom made no distinction between television and reality: if it was raining on TV, she'd ask Dad to close the windows in the house. If it was August and the TV showed a snowstorm, she'd be amazed to realize it was snowing in the dead of summer.

Chapter Five

Almost A Doctor

My mother had always been an avid reader of *Prevention Magazine*, and liked to refer to herself as an A.A.D., which, she explained, meant "Almost A Doctor." She was very well-informed about the latest reports on nutrition, diet and exercise, and was extremely strict with herself about what she ate: years and years of egg-white omelets, dry whole-wheat toast and low-fat everything. Interestingly, as Alzheimer's began to change her behavior, one day she abruptly reversed her dietary habits, and began *only* eating the egg yolks, discarding the whites. She also began eating a lot of chocolate candy and potato chips before dinner, which was unheard of in our household. I guess she was finally busting out of her long life of great self-discipline and deprivation.

It is a known fact that Alzheimer's often *does* change one's appetite and taste buds. For decades, every night after dinner, Dad was in the habit of offering Mom a cup of tea, and every night she would say "Yes." Yet now, every night she would take one small sip of the tea, make a face, and say, "Something's wrong with this, it doesn't taste right." Despite the old adage of not continuing the same behavior and expecting a different result, Dad continued to make her tea every night, and throwing it out every night in frustration, complaining to us about it, until one evening, in a moment of sheer inspiration, Harry suddenly announced,

"I just got it!"

"What?" We looked at him expectantly.

"Mom. Does. Not. Like. Tea. Anymore."

It seemed like a stroke of genius, a profound insight that opened our eyes, and my father and I marveled at how obviously true it was, astounded that we had missed seeing what was right in front of us for so many months.

Along with her careful diet, my mother had also spent years religiously swimming laps at the pool three times a week and going on frequent walks. She took great care of herself and always appeared to most people to be fifteen years younger than she was, and quite attractive and beautiful. One day, long before the onset of Alzheimer's, she was sitting on the bottom bench of the sauna at her local health spa, listening to the half-dozen ladies sitting behind and above her, speaking at length about "how ugly Jewish women are." My ballsy mom stood up and faced the women, turned around in a circle as she stared down at herself, and then announced, "It's funny, I never really considered myself to be ugly."

Fast-forwarding to when she was ninety-four, and finally reduced to a state of near total oblivion, unable to walk, talk or literally do anything at all, she remained otherwise physically healthy, and she had very few wrinkles on her still-pretty face. Witnessing her being so helpless and removed from this world, we couldn't help but wonder if her lifelong commitment to health and longevity turned out to be a very mixed blessing, condemning her to survive twenty years of steady decline when most others in worse physical shape, with co-morbidities, would surely have succumbed far earlier.

She was likewise well-read on the increasingly ubiquitous subject of Alzheimer's disease, both the signs to look for and the brain exercises one should practice to avoid it. She and my father memorized the names of the nine Supreme Court Justices and took great pride in repeating them back to one another, a way of reassuring themselves that they weren't losing it. In their eighties, they would occasionally visit nursing homes as "tourists," and made a pact that they would never put one another in such a place, "with all those old people." And they never did.

Given how much she knew about Alzheimer's, and how afraid of it I knew her to be, it wasn't surprising to discover that her default response to some very obvious symptoms was utter denial. Equally surprising, as I've said, was to see how my father too, at first, colluded in her denial. He fruitlessly tried to hide her condition from the rest of the world when, in fact, as time went on, it was patently obvious to complete strangers within minutes of meeting Mom that she was a bit loopy, and it was certainly obvious to all of their friends, relatives and neighbors. It nevertheless remained an open secret for several years, until my Dad finally recognized it had become impossible to hide her condition any longer.

I came across an old email from my father that illustrates this:

This past week Mom was again very upset Monday and Friday morning when I went walking with my friends. I think she feels that maybe I won't come home when I leave. When I got back Friday she was very angry and left the house. I was sitting at my desk and I guess she had decided to drive to the mall. At first she went out and came back immediately to say that the keys didn't work; she had taken the house keys instead of the car keys. I gave her the correct ones and I heard the car back out of the driveway and into the street. Then I heard her honk the horn repeatedly until I went out to see what was wrong; she said that the car would only go backwards! The next time she tried to take the car, she did so with no keys at all, but just banged on the steering wheel, shouting, "It's broken!" I finally realized that her driving days were over. And I guess I will also have to stop my daily morning walks for now, but I am not sure what excuse to give my cronies. The truth would circulate too fast I'm afraid. At any rate, no answer is required but thanks for listening. And, as you know, as my old army pal Curly Hoffman always said, "Better Days Are Coming!"

Love, Dad

One morning, Mom came across a photo of her favorite neighbor as a child in Germany, who had lived next door. She was so excited to see her again that she ran out of the house, in New Jersey, to go over to that neighbor's house and ring the bell, my Dad helplessly chasing after her to avoid what would have been a very embarrassing situation for him.

Other times we would take her to the local indoor mall and she would enter stores and begin to chat nonsensically with unsuspecting shopkeepers, and casually choose a variety of items off the shelves and simply stuff them in her pocketbook. We would stand behind her signaling to the workers that she was "off," and we would of course return the borrowed items as soon as we could distract her.

You may be asking yourself right about now,

"Hey, what happened to the silver lining? All of this sounds terrible."

You're right; it was, at times. But I want to be a "credible narrator" and not gloss over the difficulties we went through, so that the positive experiences I relate will be equally believable.

MOMENTS WITH MANYA

Sitting in the kitchen, Mom picked a particular piece of lettuce off of her dinner plate. She laid it out carefully on the table, straightened out the creases as best she could, then declared, as she pointed at the flatlined lettuce leaf:

"This is not a normal person."

(A friend would later point out that she was absolutely correct.)

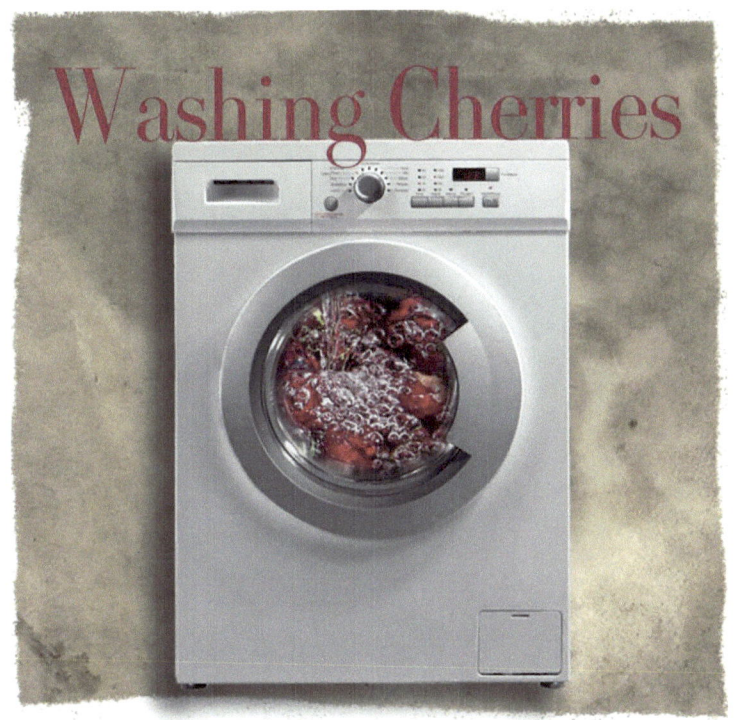

©EmbodyArt by Colormaiden

CHERRIES TO THE LAUNDROMAT?

Dad put a bowl of cherries on the dining room table for dessert and Mom picked one that was obviously rotten, and announced, "This one has to go to the laundry." She stood up and walked downstairs to the laundry room. We heard her turn the water on, presumably washed the cherry, then came back up to the kitchen, put the cherry in a glass, opened the garbage can and emptied the cherry into the trash. Then she sat back down at the dinner table, mission accomplished. We all watched with great curiosity.

Chapter Six

Manya's Story

One day, out of the blue, my mother walked up to me in the kitchen and asked,

"Do you remember your mother?"

"Yes, I do!" I answered enthusiastically, "She was German."

Mom's face lit up and she said,

"Really? Mine too! I would like to meet her someday."

"Just look in the mirror."

"You mean *I'm your* mother? Nooooo. You're kidding?"

She was completely mystified by the very idea. Then immediately uttered one of the best things she ever said to me:

"I'm glad I had you."

Ruth Manya Lerner was born in Germany, raised in a little village outside of Baden-Baden called Rheinbischophsheim, or "Bisha" for short. It has since been renamed Rheinau. Her childhood sounded idyllic to me. She spoke of ice-skating on the river over to the next village. Everyone knew everyone and would sit on their porches in the evenings telling stories and listening to my mother play her concertina. Her next-door neighbor, an ancient Gentile woman known as "The Glassemutter," would secretly give my mother forbidden non-kosher foods, like bacon, to taste under her table where my mother would crouch in waiting. She shared a bedroom with her beloved grandfather and loved going for walks with him. She had a photo of the two of them that she cherished. The surrounding Black Forest area was gorgeous. I like to imagine her as a carefree little girl, roaming the surrounding countryside without fear, enjoying the brooks and streams, and as the oldest child, helping to watch over her younger sister and brother, Gerda and Norbert.

And then, of course, the world turned upside-down and what was idyllic very rapidly became an unthinkable nightmare. Going to school each day became a terrifying ordeal for her, just as it would be for me one day when the time came, never understanding that I was unwittingly replaying an inner script of fear I had inherited from her. Many years later I took her to see the film *Cabaret,* and it included a scene at an outdoor café in which a young boy in a Nazi uniform spontaneously stands up and begins singing a patriotic song, "Tomorrow Belongs To Me," and within minutes most of the people in the café stand up and join him, their hands raised in the Heil Hitler salute. My mother's face turned ashen white, reliving a terror and horror that lived in her on a cellular level.

Manya with her Grandfather Israel

Manya's father, my grandfather Bernard Lerner, saw what was coming and decided to get himself to America and make arrangements for the rest of the family to join him once he was settled. He departed Germany in 1938, carrying a single diamond in his pocket and little else. Once in America, he gravitated toward the Diamond District on 47th Street in New York City and managed to sell his one gem at a profit, which he used to purchase several more. Formerly in the textile business, by the time I knew him several decades later, he was earning a successful living as a freelance, traveling jewelry salesman, making house calls. He often stopped by to have lunch with my mother and me during his workday and he always had a piece of rolled-up, velvety red fabric with him that he would spread out on our kitchen table to show my mother his latest collection of diamond rings, watches, bracelets and earrings.

By 1939, my grandfather had managed in just one year to convert that single diamond into sufficient funds to establish himself in Paterson, New Jersey, and had obtained visas for my mother, her siblings Gerda and Norbert, and of course his wife, their mother—my grandmother—Fanny Lerner. But they were devastated to learn that he had not succeeded in getting a visa for my grandmother's mother, who had lived with them for many years.

Her name was Elise Grumbacher; I was named after her.

It was with a heavy heart that they followed Elise's orders when she insisted they all get out of Germany while they could, and they very reluctantly left her behind. Within a year, Elise would be taken away by cattle-car to a labor camp in Gurs, France, where she would perish after only a couple of months in the unlivable conditions. The shocking grief of this turn of events would haunt our family, and my grandmother in particular, forever. Fifty years later, on her deathbed, my Grandma Fanny would often utter only two words, over and over and over again: "The Hitler, the Hitler." She never forgave herself or made peace with abandoning her mother to the Nazis, and her sorrow permeated through her very pores into my mother's psyche and subsequently into mine, like a genetic disease passed from one generation to the next.

Obviously I had no way of knowing that I was literally born into the ongoing paroxysms of grief and terror that my mother's family and the whole world had only recently experienced. Their sorrow and fear infused the very air of the first breath I took; I was infected by powerfully difficult emotional states from the moment I was born. In my novel, *Minyan: Ten Jewish Men in a World That is Heartbroken,* I only half-joked,

> *I was the world's first paranoid baby.*
> *And I've been afraid of everything, ever since.*

They call this "Second Generation Survivor Syndrome."

On the evening of Kristallnacht, the "Night of Broken Glass," November 9, 1938, the Nazis went on a rampage all over Germany, destroying, looting and setting fire to Jewish shops, homes and synagogues, and taking 30,000 people into custody, destined for concentration camps, and murdering many of them that very night. One of my grandmother's "best friends" literally threw an axe through the glass on her front door, landing at my grandmother's feet. Family lore has it that my grandmother calmly picked it up and handed it back to him, saying, "I believe this belongs to you?" By then, their non-Jewish friends and neighbors had come out of their homes and converged on the man and chased him away. But not before he and his cronies had set fire to the small, local synagogue right across the street from my mother's home. Later that night, my grandmother, a true hero, picked her way through the burning embers and located three untouched sacred Torah scrolls that she hid, initially, and eventually donated, bringing one of them to America and giving it to Temple Emmanuel in Paterson, New Jersey. My parents and I went there many years later to try to retrieve it, and it was nowhere to be found.

I was born in Paterson in 1952, and grew up nearby, in the very safe, suburban neighborhood of Fair Lawn, New Jersey, on a quiet dead-end street, enmeshed in a lifestyle perhaps most accurately depicted on the popular television sitcoms of those years, *Leave It To Beaver,* or *The Donna Reed Show.* If you don't know those shows, think '50s America, with a working and loving, wise dad; a stay-at-home, devoted housewife mom; and two mischievous kids getting themselves into trouble and then learning a valuable life lesson at the end. Those shows never had even a hint of violence or evil.

And yet in our own personal version of *Leave It To Beaver,* there was one crucial and singular difference: when our father went away on work-related trips, my mother would keep an axe under her bed. Needless to say, this completely terrified me. I had thought we were perfectly safe, but apparently Mom needed a weapon readily available to defend us against potential attack, possible intruders who could break down our door and do us harm in our own beds. I was somehow transported from *Leave It To Beaver* to a dangerous European warzone, where I had to lie awake each night, listening to every sound outside my window, intensely vigilant and on guard, my heart pounding in terror. It was an extremely frightening and unpleasant way to live. I truly felt myself to be in no less danger than Anne Frank must have felt, constantly fearing discovery and subsequent unspeakable horror.

All this was going on inside me while on the outside I went to Cub Scouts, Little League, and did my best to act like a regular little kid, so nobody really took notice that something was not right with me on the inside. I think my family gradually caught on, however, when I began lying in bed each night and screaming a single word at the top of my lungs in a short, clipped, ear-splitting burst of sound:

"SCARED!"

I would repeat the scream at regular intervals, perhaps once a minute, or more often, much to Harry's exasperation and annoyance as he was trying to sleep in the bed two feet away from mine. This would usually occur in the middle of the night, so while Harry loudly whispered, "SHUT UP! SHUT UP!" eventually my mother would rouse herself from her bed across the hall and virtually sleepwalk into our room, climb into bed with me, roll over, face the other way and fall back asleep, leaving me still wide awake, still terrified, but with no further options.

I pondered that axe under Mom's bed over the years, as it gradually dawned on me that having it there wasn't actually normal behavior. My friends' mothers, I learned, kept no weapons near their beds when their husbands were away. It wasn't until I was well into my 30s that my mother's kid brother, my Uncle Norbert, finally explained it to me. I told him about it, and he said, "Oh, you know where that axe came from, don't you?" I didn't, and he told me the story of what happened at the family home in Rheinbischophsheim on Kristallnacht in 1938.

As it turns out, my mother hadn't even been home the evening when the incident occurred, yet that axe nevertheless metaphorically traveled within her psyche overseas and over time, reappearing several decades later underneath her bed in Fair Lawn, New Jersey. How was I, as a kid, able to make sense of the contradiction between a life that appeared to be completely safe, and the need for an axe to protect us from Nazis that might show up to get us at any moment? Obviously, I *wasn't* able to make sense of it, and my internal consciousness became a confusing and scary mix of distinctly opposing realities. A psychological warzone all its own.

My mother's family departed Germany on what would prove to be the very last boat that Hitler permitted to depart for the United States, the *Bremen*. And in fact, Hitler changed his mind part way through the ship's journey across the Atlantic, and the captain was ordered to turn around and head back to Germany. Although it is next to impossible to notice a ship turning around at sea where there is no land in sight to serve as a reference point, my mother, who was 15, *did* in fact notice the change in direction. She informed my grandmother, who subsequently tracked down the captain as he strode around the main deck of the ship. When he heard what this woman's daughter had told her, his jaw dropped, and he said, "I want to meet this girl!"

In the end, the captain decided he was close enough to New York waters to disobey Hitler's orders and complete the journey to the United States. And that's how my mother, and therefore I, wound up in America.

**Manya in the center, flanked by siblings Norbert & Gerda,
and her mother, my Grandma Fanny, in the rear, arriving in America.**

©EmbodyArt by Colormaiden

"BE HERE NOW!"

Mom was so "in the moment," she would make every meditator jealous!

I called her one day:

"Hi Mom! What are you doing?"

"What am I doing? I'm sitting here with a phone in my hand."

"Really? Me too!"

"You're kidding?"

"No!"

She was amazed by the coincidence; what were the odds we were both doing the exact same thing at the exact same time?

Chapter Seven

Uncle Norbert

Mom's younger brother Norbert also got Alzheimer's. He had always been our favorite uncle. When Uncle Norbert babysat for Harry and me, he helped us build really cool forts and tunnels using all the living room sofa cushions and furniture on which we ordinarily weren't even permitted to *sit*. He knew how to make bunny rabbits out of cloth napkins, and could create a haunting flute sound by blowing through his hands. Norbert could throw a baseball so high up in the air it disappeared from view, seemingly piercing the earth's atmosphere. He was able to leap over young trees with me riding piggyback and was famous for his "rides": a hundred variations of throwing us in the air and twirling us around, or lifting us up while we hung on to his bent forearm. You know, *that* kind of uncle, the cool one, who "got" who we kids really were, surrounded by adults who generally hadn't a clue.

One night when Norbert was watching Harry and me, we all gorged ourselves on fresh-cracked pecans, and Norbert boldly declared:

"You know what I would do if I had a million dollars?"

"What?"

"I'd buy a million pecans."

It wasn't until Harry and I were well into our 40s that it suddenly dawned on us that if you did the math, his statement implied a cost of one dollar per pecan!

He also informed us that were he ever to become president, the first law he would enact would be to ban automatic faucets in public restrooms that turn themselves off as soon as you move your hands away. He was a very funny, and fun person, and I have a vivid memory of being in a car with his whole family—his wife and three kids, my cousins—leading the clan in a rousing sing-along, a type of joyful expression that I was unfamiliar with on our own family car trips. Although, on very rare occasions, we *were* able to cajole our dad into doing his famous rendition of "Tutti Frutti." (The Slim & Slam version, not Little Richard's.)

Harry and I speculated that by marrying our Aunt Karin, an easy-going, cheerful non-Jew, and moving five hours away from everyone else, Norbert was somehow the one family member who managed to escape the heavy veil of suffering that seemed to have been imported from Germany. He was also the youngest when the family emigrated, so perhaps he had not fully experienced or comprehended all that was happening.

Norbert responded to the early signs of his memory loss very differently than my mother. Whereas she would ultimately remain in denial throughout the entire process of her transition away from reality into her own mysterious world of Alzheimer's, Uncle Norbert was open and straight about it from the very beginning:

"The way I look at it," he once told me, as I happened to observe him taking his Aricept one morning, "is, why the hell should *I* care if I can't remember a bunch of trivial crap?" And by "trivial crap" he meant things like those three random words neurologists typically ask patients to repeat back to them only a few minutes after committing them to memory:

"Potato, camera, window."

Norbert couldn't make it past potato.

Or perhaps he meant the day of the week, the year, or the name of the president. He inspired me with his cavalier attitude and fearlessness. Little did he know, of course, that within a few short years, the list of "trivial crap" he was unable to remember would expand to include the names of his three children and his wife of forty-seven years, or his ability to even recognize any of them.

A highly spiritual man of non-violence, Norbert was the first person to model the behavior for me of carrying insects out of the house to release them, in an era when killing bugs was just what everyone did automatically without a moment's thought. I remember going to a supermarket with him as a child and being struck by the friendly and upbeat interaction he had with the cashier at check-out; he had a way with people that often made them laugh and brightened their day, and it was not at all dependent on their station in life. Everyone counted. I remember asking him why he said "Merry Christmas" to the cashier, given that we were Jewish, and his response was that being friendly and gracious to another human being would never be considered bad or wrong in any religion.

Norbert had met the Dalai Lama in Ithaca, New York, had taken a walk with Albert Einstein on the campus of Princeton University, and had devoured the books of Paul Brunton, whom he also eventually met in Ithaca. Brunton was a British spiritual teacher who had spent time on a pilgrimage in India, searching, and eventually happened upon and became a devotee of Ramana Maharshi, widely considered to be the greatest sage of the last century. Right up until he could no longer speak, Norbert would pull one of Brunton's books off his shelf, open it at random, and insist that whoever was there listen to him read obscure and dense passages about the nature of consciousness that still seemed to thrill his mind, heart and soul.

Yet despite this legacy as a spiritual person of humor and peace, one day Norbert spontaneously tried to strangle a bus driver on his way to Adult Day Care. And soon after he lashed out and struck my Aunt Karin as she tried to help him in the shower, and that was the turning point. He wound up spending his last years in a quiet and clean facility near his house, where Karin could visit daily, as he continued to decline into that no-man's land of end-stage Alzheimer's. The last few years he needed to be lifted in and out of bed with a Hoyer Lift, a type of crane used in those settings, and spoon-fed his meals. He had lost his ability to walk and talk, and like my mother at the end, mostly stared into space. When he very occasionally flashed a momentary smile, everyone was thrilled to see that tiny, brief flicker of aliveness shining through, because otherwise toward the end he appeared to be completely oblivious to anyone's presence. His own son, my cousin David, told me he couldn't visit him anymore, "Because that's not my Dad in there; my Dad is gone."

Several years prior to entering the facility, Norbert joined our family in a celebratory dinner on the occasion of my niece Julie's graduation from Cornell. Like the rest of us, Julie had grown up being entertained by Norbert's many "uncle tricks," especially the magic napkin bunny, which would dissolve and disappear when an unwitting child pulled on its nose. He had tried to teach all of us how to make the bunny at one time or another, including Julie, and that night, as a new Cornell graduate, Julie sat at the dinner table in a fancy restaurant and for the very first time in her life, proudly succeeded in making her very own napkin bunny. We all watched with curiosity as Uncle Norbert pushed his chair back, got up with difficulty, and began a slow-motion journey of hobbling from his end of the table over to Julie, where he leaned over and whispered to her, "The bunny's getting old," and then returned to his seat. It had taken Julie some 22 years to finally master the bunny, but the Master had spoken, and declared she was too late! Julie's mouth dropped open, completely stupefied. It was quintessential Norbert.

Soon after, he and Karin attended my parents' 60th Anniversary gathering, and cousin David told me he had to intercept Norbert coming out of the Men's Room, headed back into the party with his pants around his ankles. I later wrote Dave about the following incident with my mother:

She was standing directly outside the upstairs bathroom, and called out to us downstairs,

"Where's the bathroom?"

I shouted back,

"Directly to your right, Mom."

What I had overlooked, however, was that *directly* to her right was actually a laundry hamper, just outside the bathroom door. I watched my mother open the hamper and rummage through the dirty clothes, then shout downstairs,

"I don't see a bathroom in here."

Cousin Dave emailed back: "When your mother was looking through the laundry hamper for the bathroom, did she by any chance come across my father's car?"

We were not laughing *at* our parents; we were laughing at the whole hilarious and absurd picture; maybe it was a form of gallows humor to cover the sorrow and tragedy of it all, but it certainly wasn't only that. We had both inherited Norbert's sense of irreverent humor. As for my Mom, she always fully joined in our laughter regardless of what triggered it, and laughing together as a family is a very wonderful and joyous shared activity, one my mother enjoyed most of all.

About fifty friends and relatives gathered for my parents' 60th Anniversary party, and my mother appeared to be a happy, social butterfly, going from table to table, chatting appropriately with everyone, having a great time, appearing completely normal in many ways. But in the car on the way home, in order to not-so-subtly demonstrate to my father the truth of her condition, I casually asked, "Did you enjoy the party, Mom?"

This was literally five minutes after leaving. "What party?" she answered, which is the response I expected, but it still shocked my father, who still couldn't wrap his head around my mother's state of mind. Talk about living in the moment.

If I left her in the living room to go to the kitchen for a few minutes, when I returned we would have a joyful reunion as if I had just arrived after a long separation. She was so happy and delighted to see me each and every time. Her day was filled with such happy, unexpected surprises. Harry, speaking from his training as a psychologist, explained that it was a bit like the notion of object permanence, a skill that infants lack, thus enabling adults to play peek-a-boo just by covering their faces for a few seconds, then magically reappearing, repeatedly causing the child to howl with surprise and delight.

A similar example: We were seated in a restaurant and my father escorted Mom to the restroom. When they returned and discovered me sitting at their table, her eyes lit up and she burst out laughing, so unexpected and unlikely was it that I would be there, in the same restaurant at the same time and we'd run into each other. Several years further on in her progression, she truly *was* like an infant playing peek-a-boo; I no longer had to leave the room, I could just move a few inches out of her line of sight, then re-establish eye contact and she would smile broadly and be thrilled to see me all over again. We would do this dozens of times a day.

When I was fourteen, Norbert introduced me to my first corpse, his father's, my grandfather Bernard. At the funeral parlor, he invited Harry and me to join him in a back room before the service began, to officially identify the body. Norbert very matter-of-factly, without a sign of either fear or sorrow, simply placed his hand on my grandfather's cheek and explained, "It's cold; the body gets cold." It was a vivid moment I'd never forget, and was a powerful demonstration to me that death was nothing to be afraid of.

When he himself was near the end of his life, I was privileged to join his daughter, my cousin Ellen, in being with him at his bedside for his last twenty-four hours. As a strong believer in Eastern ideas of what might occur for the soul at the time of death, he had left clear instructions with Ellen some ten years earlier that when the time came, he wanted no morphine in his system that might cloud his consciousness and possibly interfere with his natural process of transition. Thus, for over twenty-four hours we watched him endure the non-stop strenuous and painful gasping for breath that a little morphine would have easily alleviated. Meanwhile, I held my iPhone to his ear, playing him the sounds of the ocean with the voice-over of Sogyal Rinpoche, a Tibetan Lama he had read and admired, gently guiding the transitioning soul to "Let go and relax into Natural Being."

When he finally expelled his last breath, his final exhale truly sounded like an orgasmic sigh of ecstatic relief. As one of my early spiritual teachers, Ram Dass, often quoted, "Death is like taking off a tight shoe."

Typical of the trickster he had always been, Norbert died on his birthday at the age of 81.

Norbert and Manya

Who would ever have thought his older sister, suffering a similar fate, would soldier on all those additional years? At ninety-five, like Norbert at the end, Mom was utterly oblivious to the outside world, unable to move a muscle by herself, and received round-the-clock intimate care from our angelic live-in aides, her life reduced to eating, sleeping, getting cleaned and changed, and staring. Her smiles of connection and recognition, which lit up our lives for so many years, had at last become more and more rare and fleeting. Of course, they were all the more precious when they *did* occur, as if we were receiving an important message through the very veils of reality, a moment of connection from deep inside her mysterious world to ours. It was like making momentary radio contact with another dimension, then losing the signal and returning to only static.

Nevertheless, even for that single fraction of a second, the mere hint of a half-smile was sufficient to communicate that,

"Yes, I'm still in here."

©EmbodyArt by Colormaiden

HOW DO YOU PLAY?

My niece Julie, my mother, and I sat down at the dining room table with a deck of cards. I dealt each of us five cards, with no mention of what game we were playing. There was a tangerine on the table. Julie went first and put down a ten of clubs, moved the tangerine next to the saltshaker, and selected a new card. I picked up her ten, discarded a King of Hearts and Three of Clubs as a pair, representing some unknown, mysterious alliance, and placed the tangerine on top of them.

Mom studied her cards, furrowed her brow, looked down at the table, back at her hand, then back at the table again. She finally discarded a Four of Spades, reached for the tangerine, began peeling and eating it, all three of us laughing hysterically. The game went on for at least thirty minutes, my father observing and baffled.

MOMENTS WITH MANYA

When we were looking to hire our very first home health aide, the agency sent us a nineteen-year-old from Belarus who spoke little-to-no English, and remained totally silent the entire time she was in the house, just sitting there. It was excruciating. But my mother rolled with it and talked non-stop for two hours, and when the girl finally left, Mom said to me, "I can't take care of someone now, it's too much work. She doesn't speak!"

~~~~~

I was reading *Middlemarch,* and carrying the rather heavy tome with me. Mom saw it, read the title, and asked,

"What's in the box? Middle-mensch?"

Chapter Eight

The End of Personal History

Connection. Most of us fear the possibility that our loved ones will forget our names or who we are as their memory deteriorates. Even worse, perhaps, is the possibility that they will forget who *they* are. I remember the poignant stories of family members trying to get former President Reagan to grasp the notion that he was once the most powerful man in the free world. In the movie *Iris,* about novelist Iris Murdoch, her husband shows her the many beautiful books she had published, but they mean nothing to her at all, there is no glimmer of recognition whatsoever. Iris, the woman he loved and married, was, for all intents and purposes, gone, not only from him, but from herself. That is a death, a loss, that any family must grieve. But after allowing for the grief process to unfold and run its course, it can eventually evolve into the recognition of the fact that there is still a magical, lovable person who remains quite alive, but is someone very new and different.

Perhaps, as I experienced it with my mother, the new person she became was actually deeply familiar to me because the essence of her soul remained unchanged. The only thing that had really died was her history, the story, which was merely the narrative of her life with its names and places and memories. Most of us believe that those things comprise all of who we are, and rarely consider the question, "Who am I without my history or my memories? What would be left?"

What if we viewed our loved ones with dementia as if they were actors in a play on stage? Up until this point—Act One, say—your loved one has been consistently playing more or less the identical character for some seventy years or more, then abruptly exits stage right, changes costumes, and returns in a new role. The same actor has been cast in both roles, and your love and connection is to that actor, not to their ever-changing characters.

It was a tricky and difficult perspective for us to achieve about Mom, especially for Dad. Imagine how much more difficult it would be to come to that conclusion about *ourselves*. It is next to impossible for me to imagine losing that fundamental connection with myself, that familiar timeline containing all the memories that formed the tapestry of my life story that has defined me to myself and others for so many years, creating a sense of continuity, forward motion and plotline. Who would I be without my past and my personal narrative?

I don't know and I can't even imagine it. But babies can do it. They do not yet have a story, memories, or concepts of themselves stored in their little brains. Rather, they appear to be an expression of pure, conscious awareness, taking everything in, filled with wonder. Perhaps at least some of the time, that state might be true of the Alzheimer's patient as well. It's like trying to imagine a sort of afterlife while still alive, as if the self I am used to seeing in the mirror is somehow absent, replaced by someone I no longer recognize. Who *is* that? Who am I? Possibly that is why Mom went through a stage of screaming at her image every time she passed a mirror. Spiritual seekers often choose to begin and end their journey with the underlying inquiry of "Who am I?" but Alzheimer's patients do not have any choice; the question is suddenly thrust upon them, and I imagine that that moment in their process could be extremely scary and unsettling to them. I imagine it would be a very jarring sense of being abruptly dissociated from all that is known and familiar, as if the very ground beneath their feet has been whisked away, leaving them lost and adrift, strangers in a strange land. The *identical* experience that might be a startling, exciting breakthrough and liberating epiphany to a spiritual seeker would, instead, likely present itself as more of a terrifying existential nightmare to the Alzheimer's patient.

Nearly every spiritual teaching, in one way or another, emphasizes the value of being present in the here and now, neither dwelling on the past nor anticipating the future, but learning instead to "stop and smell the roses," to fully appreciate and live in *this* moment. After all, the present moment is literally the only moment any of us are ever given to experience, and this attitude has the capacity to transport us beyond the mental burdens of time. It makes for a richer and fuller way of living.

It's easy to recognize that neither the past nor the future actually exists, except in our minds, and yet they are the chief cause of both regret and anxiety; regret for things that have happened that can never un-happen, and anxiety for what may yet happen that usually never does. We actually lose our real lives in that mental fabrication of time; we miss out on the richness of life that is always occurring all around us at every moment. As John Lennon counseled his son Sean in the song "Beautiful Boy,"

"Life is what happens to you when you're busy making other plans."

I took many walks with my mother when she taught me this lesson again and again. She was hyper-aware of every flower we passed, every bird chirping above. It was almost as if I had never taken a genuine walk before. I was so used to living inside my head—lost in thoughts, plans, or rehashing a previous event—that I was quite literally missing my actual life, already-in-progress. What a precious gift our loved ones with memory loss can give us if we are open to receiving it, learning to see with the eyes of a child.

Wouldn't it be ironic if, while we are busy lamenting our loved one's loss of memory, they themselves are finally experiencing the immediacy of their lives more directly and fully, everything new and fresh? Obviously, this is shining a very positive light on what may or may not be happening at any given moment to a patient with Alzheimer's disease, but when my mother was first showing "signs," she became, as I've said, an ebulliently happy person for the first time, I suspect, since her childhood. She was certainly the happiest and freest I had ever known her to be, as if a lifelong burden had been lifted from her soul. One day she spontaneously turned to Harry and said, "I love you." He turned to me in shock and quietly said, "That's the first time she ever said that to me in my life. I wish I had grown up with *this* mother!"

Chapter Nine

Life & Death

In addition to the seven part-time aides coming and going every day from morning to night, we had installed electric lifts on both sets of stairs, put in a raised toilet and grab bars in the bathroom, and purchased a portable rubber sink to wash my mother's hair in bed.

We used an assortment of bed rails and cushions to keep Mom from rolling out of bed before she eventually transitioned to a hospital bed. My parents shared a queen-sized bed for sixty-eight years. We also got a baby monitor and a special mattress pad that would inflate and deflate all through the night to prevent bedsores. When she was still walking on her own and getting up at night, we installed a baby gate at the top of the stairs. There were three wheelchairs in the house: small transport chairs for the main floor and upstairs, and a bigger one in the garage for rides outside in nice weather. We also had several walkers, and an electric living room recliner that could raise the seated person to a standing position, saving the backs of our aides from too much heavy lifting. We had already lost several aides over time due to back issues, because once an aide finished cleaning and dressing my mother in bed each morning, it required four lifts and transfers to get her from the bed upstairs down to the recliner in the living room where she spent her day. These were:

1) from the bed onto the upstairs wheelchair;

2) from the upstairs wheelchair onto the stair lift;

3) from the stair lift onto the downstairs wheelchair; and

4) from the downstairs wheelchair onto the recliner.

To change her in the middle of the day required doing all of that in reverse.

My parents' bedroom eventually resembled a hospital room. The shelves were stacked with night diapers, day diapers, protective "chucks" for the bed and chairs, baby wipes, Desitin, A&D cream, and at least four other specialized ointments and lotions, boxes of latex gloves, and a blood-pressure cuff. The walls and doors in the house and refrigerator and cabinets in the kitchen were covered with Excel charts Shari created, tracking Mom and Dad's daily fluid intake, blood pressure, pulse, the style and quantity of their bowel movements, and various reminders to the aides, along with emergency phone numbers of friends, relatives, neighbors and doctors. There was also a printed card containing my parents' health history and various other vital information should an aide ever have to interact with EMTs at the house, which happened at least half a dozen times over the years. One of the EMTs got on the phone with me in the midst of an emergency rescue, and we discovered we had attended 4th grade together! Thank you, Marty Pelta.

Alzheimer's patients often plateau at certain levels and persist there for months or even years at a time, before taking another plunge down to a new level. One of Mom's biggest changes, having evolved slowly, was when it finally became obvious that she needed total assistance with literally everything, all day long. The phrase "total assistance" seems to imply that she was merely being *assisted* to do things that she could still do by herself with some help, but that was not the case. During those last few years, she could do absolutely nothing for herself anymore. She needed to be sponge-bathed in bed each morning, dressed, and have someone feed her all of her puréed meals and thickened liquids. The ability to swallow without choking is a primary concern in late-stage Alzheimer's patients, and the aspiration of food going down the wrong pipe often leads to pneumonia which is one of the most common causes of death for Alzheimer's patients. (Recently I read that the thickened liquid approach has been called into question.)

She had already had several bouts of pneumonia that were diagnosed by having a home-visiting X-ray technician come to the house with a portable unit. The pneumonia episodes were easily treatable with a round of liquid antibiotics, but they triggered some interesting conversations between my brother and me about life and death.

Fortunately, Dad had seen to it that they both had Advanced Directives written up when Mom was still able to understand the idea and put her signature on it. They were both very clear and explicit that they wanted no heroic measures used to prolong their lives, specifically through using respirators or feeding tubes. They also designated themselves as DNRs—Do Not Resuscitate—in the event of cardiac arrest. But Harry had heard a pithy phrase used by a physician in the world of gerontology research: "Pneumonia is God's gift to the elderly."

For someone like our mother, who Harry perceived to have less than zero quality of life, he wondered if even a round of antibiotics should be considered a heroic measure, unnecessarily prolonging her life, which he imagined to be one of great suffering. He would often state emphatically that he himself would never want to persist in Mom's state, and he intended to somehow arrange to end his own life if he were headed in that direction. Naturally, with our mother and her brother Norbert both getting Alzheimer's, we couldn't help but recognize that the two of us were a bit of a genetic crapshoot, and therefore any momentary lapse in our own memories always gives us pause. But Harry went as far as having my name removed as his medical Power of Attorney, because he feared I would allow him to live much longer than he wanted to. (Also, it should be noted that not long ago he finally located his car keys in the refrigerator's cheese drawer.)

He and I had opposite underlying philosophies that had guided our lives: I had always been the hippie, New Age wandering spiritual seeker, ready to try anything and everything wild, weird and alternative; he had a Ph.D in Psychology, and his world view was firmly rooted in (social) science and rationality. Harry questioned the wisdom of continuing to treat episodes of pneumonia, but graciously surrendered those crucial decisions to me because I had been on the frontlines for so many years, being present and managing Mom's hands-on daily care. In my mind, I knew that Harry was essentially asking the unspoken question, "Should we kill her the next time we get a chance?"

From my perspective, a round of antibiotics was certainly not a heroic measure, and when I asked Mom's visiting doctor if we should keep treating things as they arose, or instead possibly consider hospice care, she was very clear in her response:

"Your mother is not a candidate for hospice. She is not actively dying. Her vital signs are good, her blood work is normal. As long as she is like this, we will keep treating."

End of story, as far as I was concerned, especially since I didn't sense that my mother was suffering. And therein lay Harry's greatest fear: that I wouldn't sense that *he* was suffering while being trapped in some nightmarish hell realm, unable to communicate his wishes, while his crazy younger brother was telling everyone, "No, he's fine, for all we know he's blissed out in there, he's not ready to go." That's why I'm no longer his Power of Attorney.

But Mom certainly didn't appear to be in any physical discomfort, especially with the amazing 24/7 one-on-one attention and loving care she received from our incomparable live-in aide, Tamar. Mentally and emotionally, she appeared to be oblivious to both her surroundings and her own condition ninety-nine percent of the time. The other one percent were those more and more infrequent flashes of consciousness when she would make eye contact for a few seconds and offer a half-smile, or even attempt to speak, though only soft mumbles ever came out.

Mom also continued to have a good appetite, usually eating everything that was put near her lips, which prompted her to willingly open her mouth to receive the food. She would keep her lips tightly pursed when she didn't want more food. Those two little movements of her mouth, either opening to receive or closing to reject, may well have been the last remaining communication she was able to transmit, although she might just have been operating on instinct.

Max and Manya Sobel, circa 1946

Married: December 29, 1946

Manya's glamour days at modeling school.

"Connection is everything."

Eliezer's wife Shari with his parents

El and Mom

THE SILVER LINING OF ALZHEIMER'S

Mom at 88! She had never looked her age, and her skin remained virtually wrinkle-free until the end.

Max reading Eliezer's *L'Chaim!* picture book.

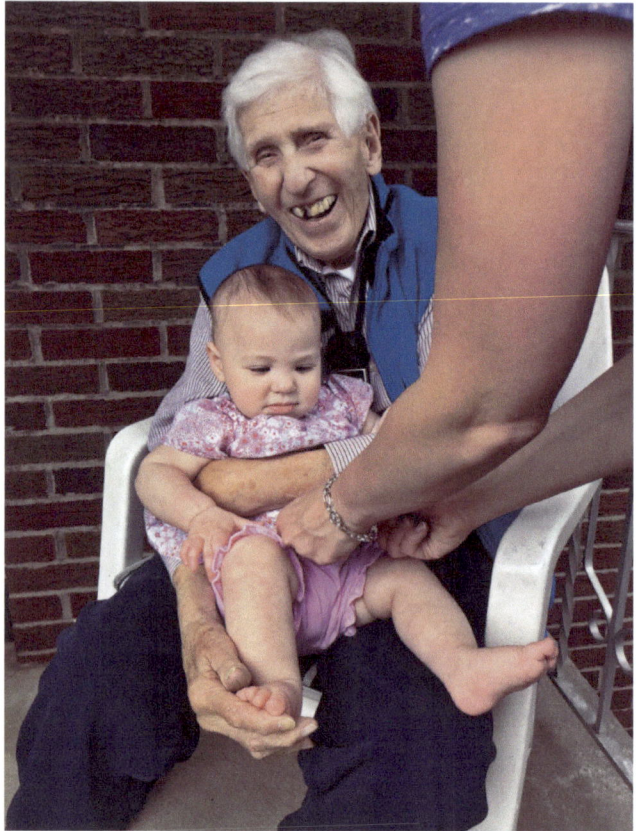

Dad meets his great-granddaughter, Talia.

(The EMTs knocked his front tooth out while pushing a breathing tube down his throat during one of many emergencies. We had to make the awful choice between the $13,000 it would cost to replace, and the actuarial tables. He would pass away five months later, toothless.)

Dad, El, Shari & Mom

The "family of origin," Harry on the right.

©EmbodyArt by Colormaiden

Do you speak Alzheimer's?

Do you ever have conversations like this:

"I don't have a pendle. I can't make the calendalish."

"Really? You can't make the calendalish?"

"Oh, you too? Well, I'll buy another aeroshpate because these are too bak. Do you have another pape to iron her? You got rid of your vindermint?"

"Yes Mom, I had to get rid of my vindermint."

"It's all ongevaltkin. You have to have somebody to noodle needle the minglemann. We had better get more bendle bissen bissen. She had a deefeleh."

Chapter Ten

Word Salad

Over time Mom's walking had first slowed to the "Alzheimer's Shuffle," barely lifting her feet off the ground. Then in the last three to five years it finally came to a dead halt. Her ability to speak, even gibberish, also eventually vanished. It appeared that she still had things she wanted to say but could no longer form any words or sounds to express them through her mouth. English had largely departed several years earlier, but at first she had generated a unique form of original gibberish that was delightful and enabled us to converse together, discussing absolute nonsense at great length, with seemingly complete mutual understanding. But within a few years there would be no more language sounds whatsoever coming from her.

It was fascinating to observe Mom's process of "unlearning" how to speak. Harry said that patients like her often seem to be reversing the way they originally learned language. For example, little children will first learn large categories of distinctions: they will come to recognize "animals" as different than humans. As their brains grow in sophistication, they will learn to further distinguish between different types of animals: cats, dogs, horses. Finally, they mature to a level where they can learn to make distinctions within particular species: collies vs. German shepherds. (Or as I learned them, Lassie vs. Rin Tin Tin.) The same process can be seen with plant life, evolving from "plants" to trees vs. bushes, grass or flowers. Finally, tulips and roses would be understood, or maple trees and aspens.

In reversing this process, we began to notice that Mom was referring to all mechanical objects as "machines." The phone was a machine, as was my video camera and the car. She knew they belonged to the same family of objects, and were different than, say, pillows, which are not machines.

Speaking of machines, one day I found her staring at the washing machine, which had just completed a cycle. I asked what she was looking for and she said, "I can't remember which button to push to dry the clothes." Before long she forgot where the laundry room was, and eventually no longer understood the word "laundry" itself. But that day, after showing her that we had to remove the wet clothes and put them in the dryer, as I was about to turn it on, she said, "Are you sure there are no children in there?"

"I'm sure, Mom."

The next stage in the devolution of her language skills was to converse in what is termed "word salad." The image brings to mind tossing a bunch of words into a big salad spinner, mixing them all up, and then pulling them out at random to create sentences. That is, she continued using English words, and the familiar cadences and rhythm of sentence structure and conversation, but more and more she wasn't making sense, and seemed to be free-associating within a rather odd stream of consciousness. Often these utterances would begin normally enough, but very rapidly devolve into the realm of word salad, as in:

"I have to see the men tomorrow, but nobody knows where they live, the fruits are all here and I think someone is going to need a horse but there's really nothing I can do about it, I'll have to ask my dentist."

I found it relatively easy to listen and affirm and respond to her, though anyone overhearing our exchange would think they had stumbled into a loony bin. Mom's next downward step in expression was to begin substituting her own made-up words for English, but still retaining the proper rhythms of speech:

"The falooternutten is never going to be okay, so we'll have to buy a mistooper later if the rindeleer man is going to frishen again."

To which I might answer:

"The rindeleer man is going to frishen again?"

"Of course! Well, nobody has an elohaipen, so that's that."

From that point it was a fairly rapid degression into pure gibberish, then eventually only sounds and mumblings, and finally the silence she lived out her days in, unable physically to use her vocal cords to form any sound whatsoever.

But somewhere in the middle of that journey of language, an amazing thing happened. Quite some time after we all assumed she had finally lost all her English language skills, one day I happened upon her flipping through a magazine in the living room, and I overheard her *reading the headlines aloud!* They were only three-word phrases in big print, but I was nevertheless totally stunned. Not only could she still form words, but she could also still *read* them, albeit only three or four words at a time.

I was very excited, and I ran out to Barnes & Noble to buy a simple picture book for people with dementia...and found nothing. I browsed through the children's section, but nothing there seemed quite right. For one thing, most of the kids' books had some sort of story to follow. For another, they were all illustrated using cartoon-like characters, and I knew my mother had a gut-level aversion to animation. I was envisioning a book that contained very simple and beautiful, realistic photographs of familiar things: people, nature, and objects, accompanied by a three-five word caption in big print. A book that would require no memory to enjoy, as each page would stand on its own as a possible subject of contemplation, or for some patients, as a stimulant for conversation with their caregivers. I wanted photos that would evoke feelings and possibly evoke memories or reminiscences, and provide people like my father with an activity to do with my mother, enabling him to share some moments of connection with her by going through the book together.

I searched Amazon and scoured the Internet, all to no avail. I was rather astonished, given the many millions of people suffering from memory loss, that I couldn't locate even a single book designed specifically for that population. I finally called the National Alzheimer's Association and was connected to their Chief Librarian, whose response to my query was, "Well, we have over 20,000 books for caregivers of patients with memory loss." To which I replied, "NO! Not for the caregiver; I want a book targeted for my mother, the patient." There was dead silence on the other end of the line. Finally, she was able to name one author (Lydia Burdick) who had published a few books for the patient. I immediately went online and ordered them, and they were very good, and our aides read them with my mother on a daily basis for quite some time, but they still weren't quite what I had been envisioning, in that they used animated illustrations and had long, full sentences as captions, as well as a simple story line to follow.

It dawned on me that there was an enormous niche market in need—millions of dementia patients, not to mention their caregivers who are always struggling, like my Dad, to find things to do with them—and virtually no resources available. I could barely wrap my head around the situation; how could this be? Nevertheless, I realized it was up to *me* to create such a book, as just one tiny drop in the ocean of what was really needed out there. And thus was my book, *Blue Sky, White Clouds* created. It was exactly what I had been futilely searching for: a simple picture book for adults with memory loss, with each page containing gorgeous and realistic photographs of familiar objects, accompanied by short captions in big print. Here are a few examples from the pages of the book:

Morton Rich

A tiny yellow bird.

Shutterstock

Snow covers the trees.

Shutterstock

The baby is fast asleep.

It was a gorgeous book, and I didn't even have to self-publish it. In one of those great serendipitous events that can happen in life, I was invited to lunch with a friend one day, and he had brought along another friend of his, who, it turned out, was Robert Friedman, the publisher of Rainbow Ridge Books. I managed to weave an informal "pitch" for my idea into our casual lunch conversation, and in a remarkable and fortuitous leap of faith, Bob essentially said, "Let's do it!" See blueskywhiteclouds.com:

Cover design by Jonathan Friedman

MOMENTS WITH MANYA

Mom had always been an impeccable housekeeper. As the saying goes, "You could eat off her floor." She kept the house neat, orderly and absolutely spotless. One afternoon, sitting at the kitchen table, I watched her very carefully corral all the crumbs from the table into one neat little pile. Then, just as carefully, she pushed the pile off the table into her waiting hand. She looked around to see if my father was watching, and when she saw he wasn't, she simply took her handful of crumbs and threw them on the floor, then cracked up uncontrollably, like a little girl with the giggles who had gotten away with murder!

Chapter Eleven

Mom's Last Vacation

In the early days before we had help in the house, when Mom was still in the earlier stages of dementia, my father would regularly call me in Virginia and put her on the phone to keep her engaged and distracted while he ran to the drugstore or to pick up a pizza for dinner. Once, I was very puzzled by my conversation with her before I figured out what was going on. She was saying things similar to her usual word salad, but there was something a bit different that I couldn't decipher at first:

"There are a lot of people here, wearing hats, and now I have all the children and it's raining. I don't know who that is, I'll have to talk to her later, but I don't know if I can help her. And now everyone is shouting too much, with all the green things, and the pickles. I have a red one and a green one."

It took me a while to recognize that there was, in fact, a method to her madness. I eventually figured out that she was describing to me, moment by moment, what she was viewing on the television screen. I could almost figure out exactly where a commercial started: "The green things and the pickles." She didn't understand commercials, because a moment earlier she might have been engaged in watching "Golden Girls," and then suddenly would see a man "squeezing the Charmin" and would protest vehemently: "Why are we watching this?" And she often confused television with reality. If it started raining on TV, she would tell my Dad that we had to close the upstairs windows. Once, in August, it was snowing on a TV show, and she said, "I can't believe it's snowing in the middle of summer."

My father's technique of keeping her on the phone with me when he went out rapidly got to the point where she just couldn't be left alone at all and he became a prisoner in his own house. He couldn't even retreat to his office to do paperwork, as she would soon come looking for him and follow him around the house, growing angry when he was out of her sight for longer than a minute or two.

We were once checking into a hotel to attend a family occasion in Philadelphia. My father and I had loaded our bags onto a luggage cart, and asked Mom to hold a side door of the hotel open while we wheeled the cart past her to the elevator, unthinkingly leaving her downstairs. We took our things up to the room and unloaded the cart. When I went back down to get Mom, I found her exactly where we had left her, still diligently holding the door open…for *nobody*. I asked her why, and she replied, "I was told to hold the door open, and I do what I am told. I don't want to get into trouble."

I reassured her that it was okay to release the door and she looked at me very warily: "Are you sure? They told me to hold it open."

"It's okay now Mom, let's go meet Dad and have some breakfast."

"How will he ever find us?"

"He said he would meet us in the dining area."

"Really? Noooo."

She was completely baffled by the arrangements, and the idea that we would actually manage to meet up with Dad amidst this strange and foreign maze of hallways in an unfamiliar building was nothing short of miraculous to her.

Some weeks later, Harry and I, along with his daughter Amy and her friend, joined my parents for a Caribbean cruise, which would prove to be my mother's last vacation or trip of any kind. Having Amy along with us was a true Godsend; in her uniquely sweet and loving way, she "got" Mom, and often held her hand

and spent time just hanging out with her and bringing her joy. She and her friend, being young and wild, enjoyed drinking at dinner and would start calling my father, hitherto known to her only as Poppi, "Dude."

On the cruise, in a new environment, we began to recognize that Mom's symptoms had grown worse than we realized. For one thing, as a foreshadowing of her anxiety about my father not being around, we were surprised to learn that even being left alone with her two sons was insufficient to curb her unease. My brother and I, along with my parents, were sitting at a table on the ship one morning, and Dad realized he had forgotten Mom's sunglasses, so went back to their cabin to retrieve them. Within minutes Mom began fidgeting and looking very nervous, and began asking,

"Where's Max?"

"He went to your room to get your sunglasses Mom, he'll be back in a few minutes."

"Maybe we should go look for him?"

"It's okay, he'll be here very soon."

"He'll never find us, we better go look."

That level of separation anxiety and attachment was new.

On a lighter note, as is the custom on cruises, we were assigned a specific table in the dining room for dinner each night, with the same waiter, and every table was filled. After three consecutive nights of this routine, when we entered the room on the fourth night, Mom looked around, marveling, and commented, "I can't believe this place is doing such a good business on a Wednesday night!"

We couldn't believe she knew it was Wednesday.

©EmbodyArt by Colormaiden

Who's Who?

An aide was walking Mom up the steps and they passed my father in his office.

"That's Max, your husband," the aide said, "do you like him?"

"Yes," my mother replied, "but I like the other one better."

Chapter Twelve

Dad's Downfall

December 29th, 2013 was my parents' sixty-seventh wedding anniversary, and roughly thirteen years into my father's full-time job as head caregiver of what by then amounted to a mini-nursing home for a single patient. Shari and I were up from Virginia to spend the New Year's weekend with a close group of friends on Long Island. We had just emerged from a snowed-in, seven-day silent meditation retreat that I had been co-leading several times a year for the previous twenty years. It had been a very happy and successful event, and we were both in good spirits, as we drove toward our friend's home.

Then my cell phone rang.

Harry was calling from his home in Massachusetts to tell us that Dad had fallen down a flight of stairs, landed on his head, and was in a Neuro Intensive Care Unit (NICU) in Ridgewood, New Jersey. Shari was driving and got off at the next exit. We continued our journey, but going in the opposite direction.

Thus began one of the most difficult nights of my life. Because my father had sustained a serious Traumatic Brain Injury (TBI), we were told that they were unable to sedate him (although in my research for this book, I found no evidence of that, so it will forever remain a mystery.) Thus, he was wide awake, utterly confused and enraged, desperately wanted to go home, and kept attempting to climb over the bed rails to escape. They were forced to fully restrain his body—legs, torso, and arms—putting him inside a living hell, and all I could do was be there with him as he writhed in mental anguish, fighting like mad, struggling against the restraints, yelling and pleading with me. He was unable to comprehend how his own son could be standing right next to him, and yet was refusing to help. One of his dearest friends in the world was there as well, a former student named Janice, who had been visiting him daily for at least a decade, and her presence just added insult to injury: his two biggest allies in the world (along with Harry, who was at home in Massachusetts) were just inches away, but neither one was lifting a finger to help him or respond to his repeated pleas for us to release him.

I served as a chaplain in a hospital at one time, and was fairly skilled at calming people down in extreme circumstances, but there was literally nothing I could say or do that would relax my father's wild desperation, urgency and panic:

"PLEASE, PLEASE UNTIE ME, EL," he implored, "WHY WON'T YOU HELP ME?"

I figured he would eventually tire himself out from the intensity of his struggle and fall asleep, but Dad remained wide awake and energized the entire night, fighting and yelling for over twelve hours.

Long night.

I asked the attending physician in the NICU if we were witnessing a life and death situation that warranted my brother making the five-hour drive from New England. The doctor (who we would henceforth refer to only as "Dr. Shrug") looked at me quizzically and shrugged his shoulders, and then after a long pause, finally said, "No, I don't think your father is in immediate danger of dying." Some hours later, in the middle of the night, after they did a C-T scan and MRI of Dad's brain and saw the extent of his internal bleeding, the same doctor responded with his signature shrug, a silent pause, then said, "Yes, I suppose you should."

We learned later from a more verbose neurologist that a fall like the one my father had would have likely killed a younger person, but since the brain shrinks with age, Dad at ninety had more space in his skull for the internal bleeding to collect.

Here's a little back story: it's both a story about Dad's *back* as well as a *back story*, as in prequel, to this horrific night in the NICU.

We had all noticed Dad's age finally catching up to him the previous few years, compounded by the daily stress of taking care of Mom. But prior to his fall and TBI, he was mentally sound enough to function normally, carrying on his complex daily life. We were especially anxious to get him to stop driving but even a subtle allusion to that notion triggered a tidal wave of rage in him the likes of which Harry and I had never witnessed in our entire lives, so we had to tread very carefully. His aide schedule was choreographed so as to allow him and Mom to be alone in the house for a quiet lunch and dinner hour together, as well as overnight. By this point Mom was taking her medication nightly and fell asleep right away and slept through the night, so Dad didn't see the need for an overnight aide, despite having had several bad incidents. Once, for example, in trying to help Mom back to bed in the early dawn hours, she wound up on the floor and he couldn't lift her and had to call Janice at 4:30 a.m. to come and help. (He also once called her at 5 a.m. to order coffee!)

Each morning when the aides arrived to begin their day with Mom, they would immediately remove the fluffy bathmat from the main bathroom, warning my father that it was very slippery and dangerous. And every evening, when the last aide finished putting my mother to bed and left for the night, my father would immediately replace the bathmat where it had always been and where he wanted it to remain. I was learning that Dad, like many of us, didn't like change, but my father's aversion to new things became much stronger as the years went by.

Sure enough, only seven weeks before his fateful fall backward down the stairs, one night while brushing his teeth the bathmat slipped out from under him and he landed on his back, breaking his spine, we would eventually learn. We had purchased a "LIFE ALERT" button for him to wear around his neck for exactly such a situation: lying helplessly on the bathroom floor, eleven at night, essentially alone because even if Mom were awake, she would have been about as helpful as a cat. It never occurred to Dad to push the emergency button dangling from his neck. Rather, over the course of several hours, he somehow managed to crawl and push his way back to the bedroom and into bed.

He saw a spinal surgeon the next day, and thankfully didn't need surgery, but wound up wearing a huge, restrictive back brace that encircled his torso like a strait jacket, so thankfully—silver lining—he couldn't drive. I took the opportunity of his recovery time to write to all of his doctors, begging them to contact the Division of Motor Vehicles (DMV) and report my father's driving.

I should mention that he had developed the frightening habit of veering wildly and abruptly between lanes on the highway and had also recently made a crash landing at a mailbox. Apparently, he had sweet-talked a Lexus dealer into doing a rush repair job on the damage so that it would look good as new when Shari and I arrived the next day. It didn't occur to him that we had eyes and ears everywhere via his seven aides. The aides, in fact, had begun parking their own cars further and further away from our house after Dad had lightly scraped against one of them when backing out.

The previous spring he had driven over a curb while attempting to park, continuing across a wide sidewalk and finally coming to a halt just short of plowing through the picture window of the Kosher Nosh restaurant, behind which an elderly couple were enjoying what could well have been their last corned beef on rye together. The sandwich was saved by literally one or two seconds. Dad's immediate reaction was to declare, "I have to get these brakes checked."

What had really occurred at the deli, however, was a mini-stroke. He needed to get *himself* checked. But like the Energizer Bunny, after just three weeks of physical therapy, he was back in action, back behind the wheel, terrorizing the neighbors, the mailboxes, and especially, all the kids who walked and rode their bicycles on his street.

Despite our repeated admonitions about not using his phone when driving, he continued to answer his old flip phone when on the road, which was a somewhat difficult operation for him even at home, sitting on a chair. I once called and he answered from the car. I heard a lot of fumbling, and then finally he said hello and asked me to hold on. I heard him call out in the background,

"What's that? Oh really? Thank you!"

When he returned to our conversation, I asked,

"Who was that, Dad?"

He answered,

"Oh it was nothing; just some guy telling me I was driving on the sidewalk."

Oh. It was nothing.

Of the three doctors I wrote to, providing them with all the evidence I just shared here, not to mention that he now had a broken spine and was wearing a full back brace, only one was willing to help, the spine surgeon. But even he was only willing to inform the DMV that his ninety-year-old patient, Max Sobel, with a broken spine, would be unable to drive for three months.

Although he completely recovered from the spinal injury in a remarkably short time, his big fall down the stairs occurred not long after, and by the time the dust settled, the DMV had responded and issued a temporary revocation of his driving privileges. They gave him thirty days to provide the information required to reapply for a new license and also required that he take a driving test. It was a letter he never saw, a response they never got, and a test he could never pass. Thus, to the benefit of Jewish delis and mailboxes all over town, my Dad never drove again.

He was essentially kicked out of the Rehab Facility where he went to recover from his spinal injury, due to his stubborn non-compliance. He was a serious fall risk, but absolutely did not "get it." The reality was, if he tried to get up by himself, the likelihood that he would instantly keel over and injure himself further was pretty close to one hundred percent. He was strictly instructed to use his call bell whenever he wished to get out of bed or get up from a chair, *for any reason*. His interpretation of those clear instructions somehow included a clause he made up that went something like, "Yes, but surely I can get up and go to the bathroom by myself, it's only six feet away." Nurses and aides at the facility were constantly discovering him all alone, strolling down the hallway with a walker, intent on getting more exercise, hoping to be allowed to return home sooner.

He got his wish: one day the physical therapist and social worker took me aside, and speaking a polite form of medical doubletalk, essentially begged me to take my father home because they didn't feel he was safe there. They couldn't have eyes on him 24/7 and he was obviously never going to cooperate. We took him home, where he had a team of visiting nurses along with physical and occupational therapists, and before long, just in time for his ninetieth birthday, Dad was once again recovered, back in action, and restored to his position as head of the household.

We were all aware that he was very unsteady and off-balance when going up stairs. He was in the habit of carrying a cup of coffee in one hand, shaking and spilling coffee, holding the banister with the other hand, and teetering like one of those inflatable clowns that you punch and it goes down to the floor and bounces up again. Watching Dad climb the stairs was terrifying, and we repeatedly pleaded with him to use both hands on the banister and let an aide bring his coffee up for him. But as I've indicated, I was slowly learning one of my father's chief character traits that I had no inkling of prior to all this: he was incredibly, maddeningly stubborn, and always insisting, "I'm *not* going to fall."

On the day of his big fall, the first day of the last three years of his life, he was returning home with a few grocery items and was trying to carry them up to the kitchen, using both arms, therefore no banister at all. An aide in the living room heard a loud thunk, and ran in to discover that the blackberries had made it up to the kitchen, but Dad was lying at the foot of the stairs, unconscious, still clinging tightly to a carton of orange juice.

The EMTs arrived very quickly, and by that time, Dad had regained consciousness and had no idea what was going on or how he had wound up on the floor. He was already physically and verbally resisting the EMTs' attempts to lift and transport him to the hospital, certain that he didn't need to go, that he was fine.

He would never be fine again. Shari and I had thought we'd be away from our Virginia home only for the seven-day retreat that had just concluded, and a second week of visits with friends and families. We had lived in Virginia for about 23 years. As it turned out, we moved into my parents' house that very night, and we never made it back to our Virginia life, ever, to this day.

One missed step. One phone call. Everything changes forever.

MOMENTS WITH MAX

Due to the decline of his hearing, whenever I called out to Shari—"Shar?"—my father would hear "Dad?" and always respond by saying "What?" and I'd have to repeatedly explain I was calling Shari, not him, which got tiresome pretty fast. As a way to make all of our lives easier, I gathered Dad, Shari and the aides together and announced, "To make it more clear when I'm calling Shari, I'm officially giving her a new nickname: 'Peaches.' So let's test it out; Shari, go downstairs." Which she did. Then I called out, "Peaches?" and without missing a beat, my father responded, "Yes darling?"

Chapter Thirteen

Becoming My Father

Following his backward fall down the stairs, my father began a ten-week stint in two different rehabs. It was very sobering to again recognize our culturally biased, inherent trust in the medical system, when in fact, we ourselves had to stay on top of his care at all times. The price we paid for that attitude was often to make doctors dislike us for not minding our own business and letting them do their work. We were the "pain in the ass" family that healthcare workers can't stand, which is not easy for a person like me who often puts being liked ahead of what's really needed.

After several weeks in the NICU, they moved Dad into a regular hospital room, and one day, after nobody responded to the call bell for nearly an hour as he lay there in soiled sheets, Harry finally went to the main nurse's station to request help. The Head Charge Nurse asked for the patient's name:

"Max Sobel," Harry replied, "in Room 2106-B." The nurse looked at her computer, puzzled, then said,

"I'm sorry, sir, there is no Max Sobel registered on this unit."

"He's four doors down," Harry said, "in the bed by the window, Room 2106." She checked again.

"No, I'm afraid not. We don't have a Max Sobel here."

"Well," Harry said, "Then who is that guy in Room 2106? He sure *looks* like my father."

Having witnessed the madness and incompetence up close, Harry realized we didn't have to play by the rules anymore. He simply picked up the phone in Dad's room, dialed the Attending Physician, whom we had never met, and said,

"This is Dr. Harry Sobel, I'd like to request an aide to come to 2106-B ASAP, as well as an oxygen unit, and I'd like to begin a round of azithromycin for suspected infection," and the Attending responded, "Yes sir, I'll get on it right away," and all of it was taken care of within fifteen minutes, for a patient who didn't even exist, according to the Charge Nurse, on orders from a "doctor" who didn't work there. And wasn't a doctor.

Eventually, Dad was transferred to the same rehab facility that had booted him out a few months earlier. This time around he was too weak and out of it to be non-compliant, in addition to which there were only about six hours, in the middle of the night, when a family member or friend wasn't at his side. His roommate had a habit of falling out of bed several times a day, demonstrating for us how the bed alarms only bring people to a patient's side *after* a fall, and so are actually quite useless in preventing injury. In fact, we learned the disturbing news that a good percentage of the patients in the rehab were there because of falls that had occurred in other facilities and nursing homes. We had our eyes on Dad every waking hour, and when it was finally time for us to go home each day, at midnight or so, we lowered his bed as far down as it would go and surrounded it with cushioned mats on the floor, and virtually buried him with pillows lining both sides of the bed.

One of us would arrive at the rehab early in the morning. One day I got there a half hour late and found him sitting in a wheelchair in the hallway, nodding off over an untouched breakfast tray. Even had he been awake, he was unable to feed himself at that point. I knew if I hadn't shown up, a clueless, though well-meaning aide, would have swiped his food tray away, cheerfully asking "Not hungry this morning, Max?" I had seen that very thing happen to another patient.

It was heartbreaking to watch my Dad, once a mathematical genius, in Occupational Therapy, trying to make change with play money and coins, and failing at the most basic arithmetic skills: How many quarters equal one dollar? If I need to change a five dollar bill to singles, how many do I get? He was also catheterized and wearing diapers for the first time ever; the overall transformation he had undergone from this one fall rendered him barely recognizable in so many ways. My father, as I knew him, was missing in action.

But not totally. Magically, amazingly and mysteriously, his sense of humor and underlying personality peeked through when we least expected it. His friend Janice and I happened to both be present when one of the rehab physicians came in to assess him toward the beginning of his stay. She leaned down close to his ear and yelled,

"MAX, DO YOU KNOW WHERE YOU ARE?"

"YES!" he shouted back.

"WHERE ARE YOU?"

"I. AM. IN. A....QUANDARY."

It was such a relief to recognize that somewhere behind the brain damage and the loss of many mental and physical functions, Dad was definitely still inside there.

"MAX," the doctor continued, "DO YOU KNOW WHO THOSE TWO PEOPLE ARE?" pointing at Janice and me.

"YES."

"CAN YOU TELL ME THEIR NAMES?"

"YES," Dad replied, clearly toying with her.

"MAX, ARE YOU ABLE TO TELL ME THE NAMES OF THOSE TWO PEOPLE?"

"THE. ANSWER. TO. YOUR. QUESTION," Dad replied, "IS YES."

At the same meeting, however, we also learned that he was under the impression that it was 1935 and Roosevelt was president. And probably due to being attended to by a pretty young Filipino nurse, he later responded to the "Where are you?" question with a reasonable guess: "The Philippines?"

As often happens in rehabs and hospitals, patients go through many ups and downs, advances and reversals. Toward the end of four weeks, my father grew extremely dehydrated, which caused increased confusion, low blood pressure and an assortment of other symptoms; he turned ash gray and was barely responsive after having made a fair amount of progress in his recovery.

We had been down this road before with both parents and knew that the simple fix for dehydration is a single liter of IV saline solution. We called the head rehab doctor to request that Dad receive a fluid infusion, and his response was to say,

"Listen, he's just going to become dehydrated again, and we can't just keep giving him fluids. I know this is hard for you as a family, but I think you need to begin the process of letting him go, saying your good-byes, and calling in hospice." In my mind I was thinking, "Yes, thank you for the straight-shooting, enlightened 'family death talk,' but I am basically asking for the equivalent of a *glass of water."* Ironically, his name was Dr. Living.

Thankfully, I was long past the stage of taking any doctor's word as the gospel truth, so I personally arranged for a private ambulance to take Dad five minutes away to a local ER. When I arrived, I had been coached by my physician brother-in-law about how to avoid the typically endless ER scene. He advised me to speak to the Attending Physician immediately, and explain that all we wanted was a simple IV fluid infusion, and would then immediately take Dad back to the rehab; no other tests, no admitting him to the hospital.

I have never seen an ER doc appear to be so delighted to help. He couldn't do enough for us to facilitate what we needed. Because it was one less emergency patient he would have to deal with and put through the routine of bloodwork, an EKG, other tests, multiple consultations and eventually finding him a room, usually after about ten hours.

Dad got his fluids and we watched him transform right before our eyes, from looking like he was one step from the grave, to regaining his color, speech, appetite and humor. Before long we had him back in the rehab, good as new, ready to resume his therapy and recovery process.

Just a glass of water.

To put closure on this incident, six months later, my father had been home for four months, was going out every day with Janice to walk around the mall, had a hearty appetite, and had regained at least seventy-five percent of his mental faculties. I videotaped him on an exercise bicycle in the living room, and on the video I asked,

"Dad, I'm going to send this video to Dr. Living, do you want to tell him how you're doing?" Waving at the camera with one hand while still cycling, Dad yelled,

"NO, I WANT TO KNOW HOW *HE* IS DOING!"

Around the same time as the dehydration incident, one of the other rehab doctors tracked me down one day, took me off to a private spot, and quietly told me:

"You really should get your father out of here, and transferred over to Kessler Institute, which specializes in brain trauma recovery. I used to work there, and I witnessed lots of people exactly like your father get better there. This isn't the place for him."

So we did. We weren't very keen on the first place anymore, not after being advised to say our good-byes and call hospice, which, as it would turn out, was premature by three full years. We moved Dad over to Kessler Institute for Rehabilitation, and when I'd visit him, he'd insist I speedily wheel him around as he fervently egged me on, "LET'S GO, LET'S GO, LET'S GO!"

I'd eventually wheel him out the front door so he could see it was about six degrees out, and the parking lot was covered in snow. This would temporarily stymie his plan of escape. I'd wheel him back in but he'd immediately begin his tirade again, this time saying, "El, PLEASE GET ME OUT OF HERE AND TAKE ME HOME RIGHT NOW! IF I DIE, YOU'LL STILL BE MY BUDDY!"

During his one-month stay there, Shari and I got busy prepping our mini nursing home to accommodate a new resident. Most of the house had already been set up for Mom, but we purchased a hospital table with wheels to serve meals on when necessary, a shower seat, and a hand-held faucet in the tub. We installed more grab bars, and a special floor alarm alongside his bed in case he tried to get up on his own, though I actually slept on the floor by his bed for the first week he was home so that if he tried to get up in the night he'd have to step on me. And one of our aides, Maria, gifted us a second recliner ejector seat from a former patient of hers.

Once Shari and I had moved into my parents' house, when Dad was still in the Neurology Intensive Care Unit (NICU), I sat at his office desk to take stock of what needed to be done. I realized that, in essence, I needed to *become* him, to assume all the duties and functions he had been performing. The extent of the responsibilities he had been comfortably handling on his own at the age of ninety totally blew me away. It was far more than I had ever had to deal with in my own life. For one thing, I discovered that his aides all had different pay scales, different pay days, and were being paid from four different checking accounts. Their random, piecemeal, hourly schedules, along with salaries and phone numbers, were scribbled on an assortment of notepads.

Ironically, the first major decision I made as I assumed responsibility and Power of Attorney for his finances, was to cut myself off. For years he had been generously gifting both Shari and me the maximum amount permitted by the IRS each year without taxation, and having my mother do the same. It amounted to quite a sizable percentage of the income we had come to rely on, but when I studied the overall picture of his financial situation, I quickly saw that he simply could no longer afford to gift us. It was a bit of a shock, because he had raised me with the mantra, "Money is no object," and it had always seemed like he had a limitless supply for all of us to do whatever we wanted. I had always privately assumed I was in line for a huge inheritance, and thus I spent my entire life not worrying about money. Seeing the actual numbers was a rude awakening; his resources, in fact, were quite finite, and with the exorbitant costs of all the private home care, his reserves were rapidly dwindling. At the age of 61, I suddenly had a nagging anxiety in the recesses of my mind concerning what in the world I might do when I grew up in order to support Shari and myself. It occurred to me that when I reached retirement age, I might have to begin working.

In the meantime, I began the task of creating simpler management systems: using one checking account, for example, and closing the rest; establishing one payday; posting an aide schedule to see at a glance who was working and when; and setting up automatic payments and online bill pay for everything I could. I was also closing out or consolidating multiple CDs, investments and IRAs with again at least four different banks—and not the same four banks that he had checking accounts with, so I was interacting with and juggling eight bank accounts at that point in my effort to simplify his finances. In my own life of semi-arrested development, I had barely made it past the ability to make change.

The tasks went on and on, involving all the aspects of running their household: managing the real estate taxes, the gardener, salt deliveries for the water softener, the underground sprinkler people, the HVAC service calls, health insurance, home and car insurance, and general repairs. I also arranged for direct deposit of his pension and both of their social security checks, and negotiated the schedule of all the visiting doctors, nurses, physical therapists, occupational therapists, a podiatrist, and even an at-home dentist for Mom at one point.

It was essentially my belated coming-of-age, as I had no choice but to step into my father's shoes after having mostly lived a childless, low-key, frugal hippie existence, generally paying no more than $150/month rent for many years, usually in exquisite country settings. I didn't marry until forty-seven. (Shari was thirty-nine, also her first marriage, and I often enjoyed introducing her to people as "my first wife.") We lived in a converted barn in Virginia with an outhouse that I built, and a wood stove as our only heat source, which meant that our winter mornings began with donning down coats, wool hats and scarves until I got a fire going. We were using water from a natural spring; whenever it stopped running, I had to climb up a mountain, then dig every three or four feet all the way back down until I isolated where the problem was.

This may sound like I'm one of those skilled, country-living guys for whom such activities are innate. But no, I am a Jewish kid from the suburbs, and since a picture is worth a thousand words, my father hung these items in the garage in 1957; I took this photo in 2019. They had never moved.

He had definitely passed his lack of handyman skills on to me. Every little successful "real man" task was, for me, a huge accomplishment. I also didn't have any of the typical adult life skills of a suburban man with a family and house. My father had helped me fill out my taxes until I was forty-three or so. To this day I don't fully grasp the difference between stocks, bonds, annuities, ETFs, IRAs, and mutual funds, or exactly what a 401K is, having never had a real job. In more ways than I like to admit, I had managed to remain a little kid in an adult body, much like that Tom Hanks character in the film *Big*. It seemed to me that for the first half of my life, the world was run by older, adult grown-ups. The second half was run by people half my age who were born knowing how to code.

Although it was never clear to us whether or not my mother had even noticed him missing for two months, the day Dad came home from the rehab was an extremely moving moment. There was a deep smile of recognition from my mother, and, still walking at the time, she slowly shuffled over to him and put both her hands on his head, as if performing a healing. Then she sat down and Dad took her hands, gazed into her eyes, and poignantly uttered, "Manya, Manya; so much happens in a lifetime."

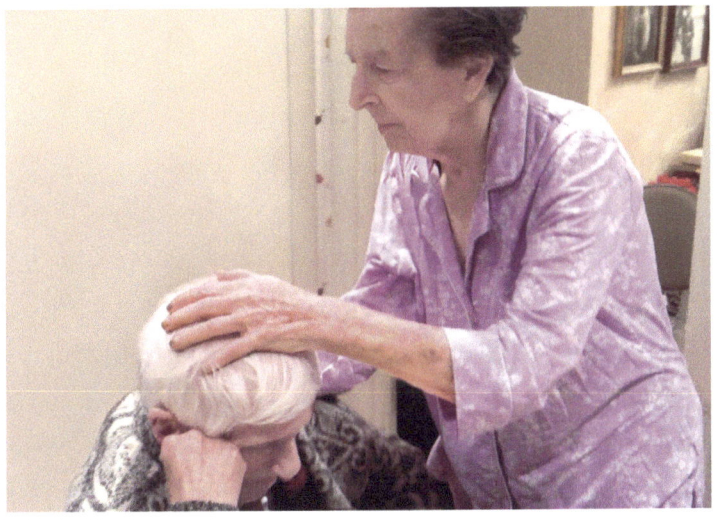

Mom's healing hands.

"Manya, Manya, so much happens in a lifetime."

Some weeks prior, we had begun interviewing people for a position we'd never needed before: a full-time, live-in aide; actually two, someone for Monday-Friday, and a weekend person. This would be in addition to Mom's seven aides. Shari and I fully intended to continue living there as well, until we felt completely comfortable with our new hires and the household was running smoothly without us.

The first person we found, through one of my mother's aides, didn't work out so well. I'll call her Tess. "The most critical aspect of this job," we explained to Tess several times, "is to keep Dad safe, by never letting him out of your sight. He is an extremely high fall risk, and he doesn't understand that. If you are not watching him, he will try to get up on his own, and will fall flat on his face and possibly hurt himself again. Do you understand?"

"Yes."

"This is more important than anything else that might come up. If you need to use the bathroom or leave the room for any reason, make sure one of Manya's aides is in the room and ask her to keep an eye on Dad while you step out."

Within minutes of the above conversation, I poked my head into the living room, and Dad was in there, all by himself, while Tess was in the kitchen washing dishes. I called her over and said, "See, this is what I was trying to say. You can't leave him sitting here alone while you do dishes. Forget the dishes, keep your eyes on Dad. He could fall any minute. Do you get what I'm saying?"

"Yes, yes, I understand."

I went downstairs, because I didn't want to stand over her on her first night and make her uncomfortable. Then I heard a loud bang. I ran upstairs and found Dad lying face down on the floor. Tess was nowhere in sight. She came in the front door a moment later; she had been smoking a cigarette on the porch. Fortunately, the soft carpeting and the way Dad fell caused him no injury. But it did cost Tess her job before she had even unpacked, and we were back to the drawing board.

Somehow through word of mouth, we got involved with the local Polish underground home health aide network. We learned about the local Polish newspaper, and responded to the ads that were in English. After interviewing a boisterous man named Krinsky with vodka on his breath, and a slimy female "agent"—more like a pimp, and dressed like one—who took two weeks' salary from "her girls" as a finder's fee, we found Adeladja, Adele for short.

She seemed perfect: bright, cheerful, efficient, and Dad took to her right away. And Adele helped us find a weekend aide, demonstrating how to weed people out from the ads in the Polish paper. She made the calls for us and we listened to her abruptly say "Dobro, good-bye," hanging up on person after person. She explained that if their first question was about the salary, she ruled them out immediately. The right person, she explained, will ask about the job and the patient first. Using this method, we also hired Dobroslawa, who said to call her Debbie.

However, what had been a smooth-running household with Mom's seven aides, gradually became a bizarre reality TV show experiment: put two new women in the picture, one of whom actually lives in the house, and suddenly we witnessed the entire dynamic shift. There were subtle power struggles, territorial disputes, vicious comments, and our peaceful home gradually grew tense and unpleasant. Adele stopped speaking to all of the other women, and we had to post a chart on the wall delineating job duties so that the household chores were evenly shared. My father was oblivious to the change in the atmosphere, and was bonding with Adele, enjoying her constant one-on-one attention and care. But we couldn't stand the tension we felt in the house. None of our interventions seemed to work, and to make matters worse, we were discovering a high-strung, hysterical part of Adele's character we hadn't seen during the interview process.

Everything came to a head at the worst possible time.

MOMENTS WITH MAX

Dad's form of dementia was not nearly as severe and complete as Mom's, but he still came out with turns of phrase sometimes that just floored us with their originality, causing us to marvel at how the human brain works. One night when we were about to wheel him from the dining room table back to his chair in the living room, he said, "We've got to go see what this prostate party is all about; let's get this pudding on the road."

~~~~~

We were a bit mystified one night when Dad came up with this tidbit: "Come on, let's take care of the fish."

We eventually deduced that he wanted to go upstairs to brush his teeth, clearing out the bits of tuna in his mouth that were a holdover from lunch. Suddenly it was crystal clear: He most certainly *did* have to take care of the fish!

~~~~~

One of Dad's more provocative inquiries:
"Is the television decaf?"

©EmbodyArt by Colormaiden

Spare Change?

I once spent an entire hour with my Mom, emptying a big box of coins on the table, and both of us moved them around, forming different shapes, stacking them, putting some back in the box, picking out the shiniest ones; there were endless things to do with the coins. My Dad was always at his wits' end to come up with activities to do with Mom, but he failed to grasp the rules of this one: "I tried, El," he told me the next day, "but she didn't know the difference between a dime and a penny."

Chapter Fourteen

"Better Times Are Coming"

The situation with Adele was escalating. By this time, Shari's mother Ann had begun to increasingly exhibit signs that she too was apparently headed toward the upside-down Land of Dementia, and her father Marty had his hands full. In order to help him, we finally moved out of my parents' house after ten months and began living an hour away with Shari's parents, trusting that mine were in good hands with our aides, despite the continuing fights and tensions among the women. We knew all of them well enough to trust that they would keep my parents well-cared for and the house running smoothly in our absence, especially since they knew we were now very involved with Ann's care.

Well, that was the case for all of my mother's aides, whom we had grown to love over the years, and whom we knew loved my parents and were essentially part of the family. But newcomer Adele—high-strung, unpredictable Adele—who had introduced dissension and conflict into the household, called me in the middle of a Thursday afternoon as I walked the aisles of a supermarket an hour away.

Adele informed me that she was not feeling well and was leaving the house to go home, right then and there. I panicked, but I knew that getting angry or demanding would only exacerbate the matter, and so I urged her to go home and rest and said I'd call her later that night to check in with her. The feeling was similar, I imagine, to having a babysitter contact you and announce she was going home, leaving your infant unattended. Meanwhile, from the produce aisle, I quickly made calls to three of my mother's aides and was saved by someone who was available to come over and take care of Dad the rest of that day, but we would have to go back and sleep there to cover the overnight shift until we had someone new. During the day we needed two aides at all times, since one might need to take Mom upstairs to clean and change her, leaving Dad alone in the living room, at great risk of getting up and falling. It was actually more than a risk; it was virtually a certainty.

When I spoke with Adele that night she said, "I'm sorry. The job is too hard for me, it's raising my blood pressure and putting my life and health in danger, and my doctor told me I have to stop." I was totally shocked to the point of being speechless. In all the years of managing Mom's care, though occasionally someone had a last-minute emergency requiring us to scramble to find coverage, all of our aides were generally quite reliable. No one had ever quit on us, let alone with no advance notice.

I pleaded with Adele to come back the following morning, a Friday, to at least give us one final day while we tried to figure something out, and also to say good-bye to my father, who had truly bonded with her in the few months she had been with us. She agreed.

I breathed a sigh of relief. At least we would have the weekend to sort things out, assuming Shari's mom had no immediate crisis, and we still had a weekend aide coming on Saturday for Dad. But an hour later Adele called back and informed me that she simply could not return to the job, not even for one day, because of her health, her doctor, her blood pressure, the list went on and on. Left in the lurch, once again I had to frantically make phone calls, and once again I got lucky and one of Mom's off-duty aides was available to cover Dad on Friday. Such last-minute juggling for coverage, apart from being nerve-wracking, was harder than one might think, since all of these women were only working part-time for us, and they all had other jobs and other patients, as well as their own families, children and responsibilities.

Saturday morning Shari and I began desperately making calls to people who had posted ads in the Polish paper. After a number of harrowing interviews with people you wouldn't trust to water your plants, let alone take care of your parents, we found Katarzyna (Katie.) Bright-eyed, kind and effervescent, she showed up with her husband, and we all had an instant rapport and connection. It was simply amazing that we found someone we loved so quickly.

Katie started working the following Monday and my father adored her. When I asked him if he missed Adele, he had no idea who I was talking about. Katie stayed with us for ten months before moving back to Poland, and apart from a few minor glitches between her and some of the other aides at the beginning, the house was by and large restored to its former, harmonious state. Katie did reveal to us, however, that one of our long-time trusted aides had a habit of viewing our back-up supplies in the garage as a free store, and regularly helped herself to a variety of items on her way home. We took it in stride, figuring that if someone was that desperate for a roll of paper towels and a bottle of apple juice, well, so be it. It was a small price to pay for otherwise excellent and reliable care.

In contrast to the lonely people we have frequently seen haunting the halls of nursing homes like ghosts, our house was always lively; at my father's insistence, we often had "parties," which meant I'd bring out my portable keyboard and, with Janice, a veteran of community theater, we'd sing old showtunes and his all-time favorite song, "Flat Foot Floogie With The Floy Doy," during which he would rise from his chair, with help, and manage to do a little two-step with his walker and a gal on each arm, while enthusiastically singing in full voice. His famous rendition of "Tutti Frutti" was another favorite, along with "Show Me The Way To Go Home," which I would eventually sing at his funeral as they wheeled his casket out of the main room. As a group, we often sang "You Are My Sunshine" to my mother, and my father loved singing an old army song, with us joining in:

> "Oh, the doughnuts that they serve us,
> they say are mighty fine;
> one rolled off the table,
> and killed a friend of mine!
>
> Oh how I hate this army life,
> Gee Ma, I wanna go,
> Gee Ma, I wanna go,
> Gee Ma, I wanna go HOME."

I've often heard people say something along the lines of, "If I ever get to the point where someone else has to wipe my butt, it's all over; shoot me."

The value of an entire lifetime is reduced to this one, necessary physiological activity of daily life. Particularly in our American culture, it somehow represents a final humiliation that makes continuing to live simply not worthwhile.

Or does it?

It was quite eye-opening to read noted death and dying activist Stephen Jenkinson's aptly-titled essay, "Who Wipes Whom?" in which he writes of other cultures and tribes around the world where the natural cycle of life is more accepted and integrated into the customs of the group. There really *are* places where cleaning and changing our elders is no more significant or humiliating than when they did the same for us as infants. The circle simply comes around, and the change in roles is treated with grace and dignity. It is not necessarily a gloomy harbinger that the end is near, and it certainly is not some Divine signal to call it quits and end one's life prematurely.

For there are clearly lots of "quality-of-life" moments that continue to occur daily for the "wipees," outside the bathroom. Holding and kissing one's grandchildren, or in my parents' case, their great-grandchildren, is but one wonderful example. There are still songs to be sung, laughter to be had, quiet moments of wordless, shared time and space; a goodnight kiss or caress; a walk or a wheelchair ride around the local park.

In a pinch I was sometimes involved in the hands-on, intimate care for my father; fortunately I had read Jenkinson's essay, the spirit of which I believe I somehow managed to convey to my dad, and he seemed to take the whole event in stride. However, I was generally more engaged, along with Shari, in a supervisory position, managing our mini-nursing home for two, but not actually doing the actual care.

An Aside: Dad's War Stories

A sergeant in World War II, Dad fought in the Battle of the Bulge and was awarded a Purple Heart for shrapnel wounds. His favorite, oft-repeated army story was about the time his unit, "The Men of Company K," entered an abandoned German home that had a wine cellar, and he got dead drunk for the first and last time in his life. His fellow soldiers literally had to carry him back to base, and when his best army buddy, Curly Hoffman, saw them carrying Dad in, he jumped up and ran over in horror, thinking that my father had been wounded or killed. When the men assured him that he was merely intoxicated, Curly looked down at him and famously said, "In that case, let the son of a bitch die!"

Dad never saw Curly again, but seventy years later he was still quoting him on a daily basis, and always ended his emails with the same words:

"As Curly Hoffman always said, 'Better days are coming!'"

Harry and I could never figure out the source of his optimism, because from our point of view, better days were definitely *not* coming; quite the contrary. But Curly's words were gospel to Dad, even though we couldn't help but hear his Curly quote as a form of utter denial of the reality of his and Mom's situation.

Looking back, maybe we were wrong. Who said you can't be a voice for optimism and hope for better days even standing on the precipice of life's great abyss?

Dad also told us about running across open fields of battle, watching friends on either side of him get shot and fall to the ground, telling us, "You just never knew which bullet had your name on it." It was very hard for me to imagine my father, a Jewish math nerd from Paterson, New Jersey, never athletic or stereotypically "manly" or strong, surviving the horrors and carnage of war, nor the psychological/emotional impact that experience had on him. If he was scarred or traumatized by it, it was not at all apparent or obvious. I guess I'm projecting. *I* feel traumatized and scarred just hearing about violence and wars. He did tell us about friends who had returned from the war "shell-shocked," the term used back then for PTSD; thankfully, it somehow spared Dad.

At one point, he told us about somehow arranging for a day's leave to briefly meet up with his older brother Sam in London, also in the army, who gave him a two-dollar bill that Dad would carry in his wallet for the rest of his life. They also created a code for their letters, which were subject to scrutiny and censure. If a letter began with just the other's name, leaving out the traditional "Dear" that would normally come first, it meant that a location transfer was imminent and they'd be out of touch for a while.

Max & brother Sam

One war story Dad often proudly repeated never made sense to me. His troop had come to a clearing, and somehow they knew the Germans were hiding in the trees just across the opening. The Lieutenant asked if anyone in the unit spoke German, and my father, having grown up in a Yiddish-speaking household, and having gotten to know my German mother and her family, knew enough of the language to volunteer. He was told to shout across the opening, in German, "Come out with your hands up, we will not shoot."

"KOMM MIT DEINEN HÄNDEN NACH OBEN. WIR WERDEN NICHT SCHIESSEN."

From the woods came a question in response:

"VAS?"

My father began to repeat the injunction, but as soon as he uttered the first word, the Germans opened fire, having confirmed the Americans' location through my dad's voice. That's the part that didn't make sense. Why in the world did his superior officer think the Germans would just put down their guns and come out, when they could just as easily shoot as be shot at?

My father actually dug and slept in foxholes, in the middle of God-knows-where. It's unimaginable to me. We never even went *camping*. He told me about seeing a soldier in a village who had been completely flattened like a pancake, as if by a steamroller. He talked about it with no emotion, as if he were describing some mundane, common sight.

Through it all, Dad managed to write his mother, my Grandma Becky back in Paterson, daily letters—"V-mail"— in Yiddish, and we also have a box filled with hundreds of daily love-letters in English that he sent my mother, each and every one beginning with, "My Darling Manya" and mostly repeating the contents of the previous day's letter verbatim.

MOMENTS WITH MAX

For quite a while when he first returned from Rehab, Dad's swallow reflex was challenged, and his doctors ordered that he only be given puréed food. A chicken dinner with a sweet potato and broccoli, for example, would come out looking like a plate of glop; or more accurately, a plate containing three individual piles of glop: a beige one for the chicken, orange glop for the sweet potato, and green for the broccoli. It wasn't, by any stretch of the imagination, even remotely appetizing. One Friday night when Harry, his wife, and daughters were visiting, Shari prepared just such a chicken dinner, and we put everyone's plates out with the food already on it and we were hoping against hope that Dad's brain injury had sufficiently impaired his awareness such that he wouldn't notice that his dinner was quite different from everyone else's. The moment he arrived, and his aide helped him to his traditional seat at the head of the table, he looked down at his plate, looked up and around the table, then back at his plate, then lifted his head and said to all of us, "Who do you have to know to get a decent piece of chicken around here?"

©EmbodyArt by Colormaiden

What Size?

Dad went to the bank today. The teller said, "Do you want a tee shirt?" Dad didn't have his hearing aids in and figured that the bank must be doing a promotion of some sort. "Sure!" he said. "What size?" the teller asked. "Medium." She took his pension check, and gave him his cash half in twenties, half in fifties. He later realized that she had seen his check was a pension payment for an educator, and what she had actually asked him was, "Are you a teacher?" not "Do you want a tee-shirt?" And when she asked "What size?" she had been referring to the size of the bills. When he answered "Medium," she gave him half in twenties and half in fifties. My friend Scott later commented, "He should have asked for a Large."

MOMENTS WITH MAX

Best conversation ever:

Dad: "What time is my appointment tomorrow?"

Me, sitting next to him on the couch: "Two-thirty."

Dad: "Well I guess I can call in the morning to double-check."

Me: "No, you don't have to double-check. I made the appointment for you, and wrote it down right here in your appointment book."

Dad: "Okay, well I guess I'll call tomorrow to verify it."

Me: (A bit flustered) "Why don't you just call ME to verify it???"

Dad: "You? Oh, okay."

He picks up his cellphone, hits the speed-dial button, and my phone rings. I answer it, sitting less than four feet away from him.

Me: "Hello?"

Dad: "El? What time is my appointment tomorrow?"

Me: "Two-thirty, Dad."

Dad: "Oh okay, thanks."

He hangs up the phone, turns to me, and says,

"You were right!"

Chapter Fifteen

Shari's Mom

Shari's mother Ann had been living some years with what we suspected was Lewy-Body dementia, which can look very similar to Alzheimer's on the outside, although it is in fact medically more closely related to Parkinson's disease. Along with the familiar signs of dementia and memory-loss, Lewy-Body also often provides patients with the added bonus of vivid hallucinations and, in her case, something called "Capgras Syndrome"—pronounced "cap-grah." It is sometimes referred to as the Imposter Syndrome. In Ann's case, she believed that Shari's father, Marty, had been abducted and taken away, because she had "heard about it on television" the previous Thanksgiving, and he had been replaced by someone who looked and acted *exactly* the same, but clearly wasn't "the real Marty." In fact, Ann told us there were four such Marty doppelgängers living in the house. One day, "one of them" was under the bathroom sink upstairs, struggling to repair a leaking pipe. Ann was standing over him, watching, and said, "Should I go get the other Marty? He's a lot handier than you. I think he's napping downstairs."

(I'm reminded of a moment with my mother, who did not have this unusual disorder, but one day an aide walked her past the open door to my father's office, where he was sitting at his desk. The aide said, "That's Max, your husband; do you like him?" "Yes," my mother replied, "but I like the other one better." Maybe it runs in the family, because my father told me that when I was five years old and we moved to a new neighborhood, whenever I was upset with him I would always proclaim, "I liked you better at our old house.")

Shari's mother Ann was generally very quiet unless you engaged her, and it was only with a little active probing that we uncovered the wild world she was truly inhabiting as she just sat there and generally appeared to be mostly quite normal. But as I gently quizzed her, I learned that in addition to the multiple husbands, she also had twelve identical homes, each decorated in precisely the same way, down to the tiniest item on each shelf, or even a random piece of chipped paint on the ceiling.

The tiny computer room upstairs—no bigger than six feet by six feet—was apparently inhabited, she said, by "Twenty-six teenagers who spend the whole day washing their hair and drawing pictures of lions on the wall." Also, we learned that a large group of "Black kids" occupied the basement. It was a very crowded household. She often warned us not to sit on someone who wasn't there, usually one of her other kids or grandchildren. And she set the dinner table every night for her original family of five, though she lived alone with Shari's dad. (Unless perhaps it was for her and the four Martys.)

One cold, winter night Marty awoke to discover Ann was missing from the bed. He got up to look for her and found her sitting downstairs on the living room couch, fully dressed, including coat, hat and gloves, and she had the front door wide open. He asked her what she was doing, and she replied, "I'm waiting for the limousine to show up and take me to get my ID picture taken." Unable to talk her out of it, Marty spent the rest of that night sleeping on the floor in front of the door, so that Ann would be forced to step on him to leave the house.

I pause here to reflect: How many incredible and wacky stories like this are occurring all around the world at any given moment, given the many, many millions of people suffering with forms of dementia and memory loss? This book provides just a glimpse into one family's experience, but it behooves all of us to multiply our moments of madness exponentially. It's not hard, at this rate, given the ever-increasing number of Alzheimer's cases, to imagine our world becoming like the film *King of Hearts,* in which the insane have become the norm and the normal are viewed as aberrations, leaving the viewer to decide who the crazy ones are. As one of my early mentors, Stewart Emery, once said, "Nobody told us when we were born that we were arriving in the lunatic asylum of the galaxy!" Which reminds me of a story:

A woman was visiting her son in a hospital psychiatric unit, and when she was ready to go, a security guard at the door told her she was not permitted to leave, as it was a lockdown ward. She explained that she wasn't a patient, but had just been visiting her son, but the guard was adamant: "Wish I could help you Ma'am, but rules are rules." She grew increasingly frustrated, bordering on panic, but just then, two men in white coats approached and took the "security guard" away, saying, "Okay Mr. Dyer, your shift is over for the day, time to go back to your room."

While Shari and I were engaged full-time in managing both of my parents' care, Ann's health began declining; she wasn't eating or drinking much, and one day she just collapsed to the floor and Marty couldn't get her up. We received one of those dreaded "ER calls" which had become a regular part of our lives by then. She was admitted to the hospital for a few days and treated for a possible UTI (Urinary Tract Infection, which it turned out she didn't have) as well as the familiar culprit, dehydration, and was released to a rehab, in hopes of getting her back on her feet and able to return to one of her twelve houses.

Sadly, Ann never made it home. She contracted a potentially deadly infection in the rehab, called Clostridium Difficile Bacteria, or "C-Diff," not uncommon in nursing homes and similar facilities, and it took its toll on Ann's already fragile condition. Fortunately, we had learned our lesson about facilities with my parents, and immediately hired round-the-clock private aides to stay with Ann and watch over her at the rehab, in addition to our daily, extended visits.

Again, I am aware as I write this of our amazingly fortunate financial circumstances. Both my father and Marty had been very successful in life: Marty had been a chemist working for Colgate-Palmolive, and his claim to fame was inventing the first-ever whitening agent for toothpaste that was subsequently used in the formula for Ultra-Brite, for which he received a $200 bonus. Both he and my dad had accumulated sufficient savings to allow us to do everything we did for them. Later, after my father passed away, we remained able to pay for Mom's full-time, at-home care through his continued monthly pension and social security checks (both of which transfer to the spouse at the time of death) and miraculously, they were just enough to cover my mother's monthly expenses, almost to the penny.

We were not unaware that we were incredibly lucky and privileged to have the finances available to keep both of my parents at home with full-time home health aides, and it does not escape me that probably ninety percent of people in a similar situation have to frantically sweat and scramble to pay the astronomical costs of caring for an elder in need of constant attention and help, while continuing to hold down their own jobs and care for their own families.

My dear friend T.R. was one such person. Her mother had been caring for T.R.'s father for two years since his Alzheimer's diagnosis, and T.R. came on weekends to help. At one point, T.R.'s mom had a heart procedure that went awry and put her in the ICU for nearly a month, and her heart was never the same again. T.R. decided to move into her parents' home and make the daily 75-mile, one-way commute to her work. Her mother continued to have multiple medical crises including one that left her in a coma, an extended stint in a rehab, and several dangerous, community-acquired infections requiring further hospital stays. When they finally discharged T.R.'s mother, she was put on hospice, given a few months to live, and sent home with *five tubes* in her. When T.R. asked her the ultimate question—whether or not she wanted to continue fighting—she nodded "Yes." Her mom slowly began to improve, most of the tubes came out, and a few months turned into two years.

Across the room was Bill, T.R.'s dad, mostly confined to a wheelchair and in the mid-to-late stages of Alzheimer's. The tipping point of his diagnosis came one night when he left the house in a rage, stark naked, got in his car, and threatened to drive around and "smash things up"; fortunately, he was stopped by a neighbor. Unfortunately, unlike my mother who became increasingly softer and loving as her condition grew worse, Bill went in the opposite direction. He began using a lot of profanity and told strangers they were ugly, fat, or both. One of his favorite phrases was, "Look at the ass on that tomato." Once they found the right medication for Bill, he was happy most of the time, albeit with occasional outbursts of obscenities.

T.R. had two elderly parents to feed, clean and change all by herself: one was a bedridden person who had survived a coma, the other had Alzheimer's and regularly used profanity. However, she *was* able to get a little outside help, which enabled her to complete a writing program during all this drama. My favorite piece of hers was titled, "If You Don't Like Being Called a C*nt, This Job's Not for You."

Yet compared to many, even T.R. was lucky, in that she was able to keep her parents at home and was herself available to care for them around the clock; and amazingly, in California, one can actually get paid by the state to stay home as a caregiver. The more usual situation in most places would have required someone in T.R.'s position to continue working full-time at a job just to stay afloat, and then what? If a full-time aide is unaffordable at the going rate of $200-$300/day, a Medicaid-funded nursing home becomes the only real option for those with limited funds. Given the level of care I've already described in even the best of facilities, sending a parent to a nursing home, especially those that only take Medicaid, can often be a death sentence. (With many wonderful, if rare, exceptions.) If the government ever decided to cut back on Medicaid benefits for the indigent, we'd be facing an epidemic of homeless elderly people with dementia, in desperate need of care, often having no family members to look after them.

I remember a very surreal "family meeting" about Ann with her rehab staff. Someone from Nursing, Physical Therapy and Social Work was present, along with Marty, Shari, and me; her brother and sister, Dave and Bonnie, were teleconferenced in. The first thing I found odd was that neither the nurse nor the physical therapist at the meeting had *ever met* Ann and were simply reporting on her status from the chart, which, it became clear pretty soon, was filled with misinformation. I had to prevent myself from either bursting out laughing or throwing the table over in outrage when the physical therapist authoritatively stated, "Ann's walking seems to be improving every day," when, in fact, Ann hadn't left her bed in two weeks and was barely conscious, and was soon to enter hospice care. The nurse read us an inaccurate list of her current medications, which we corrected her on. Needless to say, the meeting did not instill confidence.

In the end, about two months following the original emergency room visit, Shari's family and I gathered around Ann for a very sweet and peaceful vigil of several days. I brought my guitar, and Shari's sister Bonnie, who has a beautiful singing voice, serenaded Ann with her favorite old Yiddish songs, and we played her favorite operas on an iPad. She mustered up a few smiles of acknowledgment and greeting at first, but gradually and gently faded into a quiet sleep, with her breath barely perceptible. At one point we thought she had passed away and called the nurse in, but she checked her pulse and said she was still with us.

It was deeply mysterious and striking to me how such a thin strand between this world and the next could be so subtle that we actually hadn't been sure if Ann was alive or dead. It was as if she had been on a very long journey and had only one final, tiny step further to go before arriving at her final destination; just the tiniest whisper of soft air in her lungs was separating her from this life and the Great Unknown.

Several moments later we called the nurse in again, and this time she confirmed that Ann had indeed left us at last, and everyone in the room burst into tears at once: of sadness, of relief, and perhaps even a tinge of joy that Ann was finally free from suffering. The "real" Marty quietly wept. He had lost his partner and best friend of nearly 60 years.

Thank you, Ann, for always making my favorite meals when Shari and I came to visit, along with your famous key lime pies, but most of all for being such an easy-going, accepting and welcoming mother-in-law, the epitome of grace, kindness and good humor. Contrary to the thousands of stereotypical "mother-in-law jokes," I never imagined when I married Shari that I had also won the "in-laws lottery," and would feel so relaxed and at home with what rapidly became my second family. Ann, may your soul be forever peaceful and free.

Shari's parents, Ann and Marty Cordon

PS: Since the time of this writing, sadly, my dear father-in-law, Marty Cordon, also left this world, at the age of 95. He was considered one of the sweetest and most generous-hearted people by everyone who had the good fortune of coming into contact with him. Of our four parents, he is the only one who fully retained "his marbles" until the very end and was still doing his own taxes. Marty was a chemist, employed by Colgate-Palmolive for his entire career, and enjoyed his fifteen minutes of fame when, as I mentioned earlier, he patented the first-ever whitening agent for toothpaste, originally released as Ultra-Brite. So next time you smile, think of Marty! In keeping with his scientific inclinations, he donated his body to science.

©EmbodyArt by Colormaiden

Breaking Your Own Rules

For someone who was always so proper, and kept an immaculately clean household, I once watched my mom very carefully collect all the crumbs from the kitchen table, sweep them into her other hand, then look around to see if my father was watching, and with a mischievous smile, abruptly throw the crumbs on the floor, laughing hysterically, like she had gotten away with murder!

Chapter Sixteen

Dad & Mom's Farewell Scenes

About six months before my father left this world, we had had to call 911 at around 1 a.m. to take him to the ER. He was having an extreme, continuous, and relentless coughing attack, during which he could barely come up for air. Our attempts to help him wound up with him on a mass of cushions on the floor, wedged between two hospital beds, utterly immoveable, and still furiously coughing. So we called and they came and took him to the hospital.

A very assuring cardiologist in the ER checked him out and informed us with great authority, "I am one-hundred percent certain that this is not a cardiac issue."

Later, following a clear chest x-ray and an unremarkable C-T scan of his lungs, the Head Pulmonologist informed us, with equal certainty, "This has nothing to do with his lungs; it's *definitely* a cardiac problem."

Here were some other possible causes of his distress that we were offered:

- His Primary Care doctor conjectured that he had a sudden case, at ninety-two, of GERD—acid reflux—and prescribed Nexium.

- The hospital speech therapist administered a swallow test, which he passed, yet she concluded he was most likely aspirating food, causing the cough, just not enough to show up as aspirational pneumonia on the scans.

- A second cardiologist declared he most likely had had a "silent heart attack"— the kind that doesn't make any noise, I guess?—several months back. When I told him that his colleague was "one-hundred percent certain this wasn't a cardiac issue," he responded with a roll of his eyes, and said, "Well, I would be considerably less certain than that."

- A third member of the cardiology team, who we later learned was a "Fellow"—and a jolly good one, at that—spent forty minutes enthusiastically, even gleefully, describing the procedure he intended to perform the next morning, coming up through Dad's groin with a catheter, to look around in his heart, possibly to install a stent if he discovered any blockages, but mostly to scout the terrain for a valve replacement to follow several weeks later.

Doctors with a medical fellowship need to practice their surgical skills to gain experience, so they tend to push for these things. Fortunately, when he observed Dad coughing his head off in the bed, he remarked, "Of course," changing his tune from eager to hesitant, "your father would have to be able to lie flat, cooperate, and not cough for several hours."

Oops.

"And you would also have to remove his DNR (Do Not Resuscitate) or we won't do any procedures on him at all." Hmm. So, we were supposed to undo my father's stated wishes, made when he was of sound mind, defeating the whole purpose of an "Advanced Directive." And this would be to do a procedure on a man who had recently had a brain injury, a stroke, and a major seizure; a procedure, we later learned, which carried the risk of stroke, heart attack and death. Even a minor cold had a very noticeable and rather instant negative impact on Dad's cognitive status and levels of confusion. Imagine what a surgical procedure would do to a ninety-two-year-old with those conditions? We said no.

Thankfully, Marcus Welby finally showed up. The older/wiser Head of Cardiology came to meet us and, to our surprise and relief, totally agreed with our decision not to do any invasive procedures, for all of the above reasons, in addition to the following, which was rather eye-opening:

"We really have no idea if his heart has anything to do with his coughing fits, nor if the procedure would help in the slightest."

Now *that* was food for thought.

We had noticed that when the EMTs had arrived at the house and placed an oxygen mask on my father, his five-hour coughing fit stopped instantly. We concluded that getting him discharged with at-home oxygen might be a good idea.

Easier said than done. His saturation levels in the hospital, having been on oxygen for several days, were well above the level that would qualify him for at-home oxygen. Once again, Harry, using his Ph.D "Doctor" title in an enterprising manner, managed to juggle Dad's oxygen numbers on his chart, and thankfully, we got him home, with oxygen, in one piece, his symptoms abated. But in the end, congestive heart failure was, in fact, the agreed-upon diagnosis.

He managed to squeeze another six months of life out of his failing heart. He continued to receive physical therapy at home and walked several daily laps around the living room-to-kitchen-to-dining room loop, always with someone holding onto the back of his pants in case he lost his balance. He was on diuretics, and at one point developed "Bullous Pemphigoid," a condition that manifests as grotesquely large, horror-movie style, golf-ball-sized blisters covering both of his swollen feet. A healthy dose of Prednisone steroids cured him, and we discovered a well-known side effect of that drug: Dad became euphoric. Throughout his life my father was generally upbeat, and certainly never a depressive type, though in the last few years he had developed a less positive affect and outlook as his abilities and mobility decreased and he found himself spending more and more time just sitting in the living room with Mom, with whom he could no longer converse.

Shortly after his first few doses of Prednisone, however, when I made my daily check-in call to ask how he was feeling, he replied,

"El, I am so blessed and so very content. I'm surrounded by great people, Mom is here, they feed me and take care of me, I couldn't ask for more." It was a striking departure from his general demeanor at the time, and the only downside was that all of his physicians agreed that he should not stay on the steroids any longer than necessary, and he would have to be tapered off them slowly. When we saw how rapidly his mood declined along with his Prednisone dosage, his cardiologist agreed that given his age and circumstances, we could try keeping him on the drugs. Unfortunately, the euphoric effect never returned, and we returned to tapering him off.

It is a known medical fact that Prednisone must be reduced very carefully and gradually. We had his precise dosage prepared in a daily pill box. What we failed to recognize, however, is that our most recent, and final, aide for Dad turned out to be nearly blind when it came to seeing things up close. On what would become a fateful day, he failed to see the second pill in Dad's meds container, thus giving him an abruptly lower dose of Prednisone than his tapering process called for. We're not certain, of course, but it's quite possible that that "medical error" killed my father.

There is a famous line from the film *Little Big Man*, when a Native American wise elder tells a young and confused Dustin Hoffman, "It's a good day to die." Then he calmly and peacefully lies down on the grass, under the sky and clouds, and patiently awaits the end, which, alas, doesn't come as anticipated. Thus, he had yet another day ahead of him, which, it can be presumed, would be a good day to live. Or die. Like the rest of us.

Is it ever a good day for a father to die? Actually, in Dad's case, I think the answer might be yes. If I had to design a death scene for him, I couldn't have made it much better. It happened on a Friday, and as fate would have it, it was Veteran's Day, November 11th, 2016. My father had literally been admitted to at-home hospice care only two days before. Earlier that week, on Monday, his aide called to tell us that he couldn't, or wouldn't, get out of bed. This was a major red flag, because until that morning, Dad had never spent even a single day being bedridden in the three years since returning home following his Traumatic Brain Injury and two-month rehab stint. (And actually, I don't recall him ever bedridden at home in his entire life.)

On Dad's last day with us, Harry was en route, making the five-hour trip down to New Jersey from his home in Newburyport, Massachusetts, and it was as if Dad was waiting for him. He spent the morning in bed, as he had for the previous four days. Janice made her daily visit and fed him lunch, then left to run some errands. When Harry showed up, Dad almost immediately entered a state of labored breathing and briefly endured some suffering, but compared to the many deathbeds I had sat beside as a hospital chaplain, it was minimal. Meanwhile, I was scrambling somewhat frantically on the phone with hospice to get instructions about how much liquid morphine to administer to him. They also instructed me to crush some Ativan in honey and put it in his mouth, the only way to get a pill in him. The combination of those two medications, in very minimal doses, allowed his body and breathing to relax, and then very gently and subtly, with Harry and me on either side of him, speaking to him, while holding both of his son's hands, in his own bed at home, he seemed to just peacefully drift off and fade away, as if to sleep, and left this world.

An hour later, as we waited for the funeral home to come and take Dad's body away, I was sitting in the living room, and Harry was upstairs saying his final good-byes. When he came down, he approached me without a word, and held out Dad's gold wedding band, indicating I should put my hand out, and he slid the ring onto my finger. We had never discussed this, and that ring had literally never left my father's hand for nearly seventy years. It was a beautiful, silent gesture of acknowledgment from my older brother, his way of thanking me for being present with Dad for the final three years of his life. It touched me deeply; thanks Har.

We brought Mom upstairs to be with Dad's body, putting their hands together. I have no idea if my mother had any idea that he had died, or had ever existed in the first place. Harry and I opted not to have a rabbi lead the funeral service, as my father no longer had a personal connection with any rabbis as he once did for many years. We put together the funeral ourselves, and I must say, Harry and I threw one hell of a good funeral, striking just the right balance between poignant reminiscences, grief, and humor. I played my guitar and asked the audience to join me in a Jewish song that my father had specifically requested in his Last Will & Testament. I also read from some notes Dad left us for the occasion.

My father was extremely organized throughout his life. When we had to clear out his office, I found lesson plans for every class he taught for some 50 years or so. He had delivered the keynote address at my high school graduation, and 20 years later, I asked him if he still had a copy of it by any chance, not expecting that he would. Within two days I had his printed speech in my hands along with a cassette tape recording of him delivering it from that night, two decades before. In any case, in his notes to us he requested that when we spoke about him at his funeral, he wished that we emphasize his role as a husband, father, and grandfather, rather than focus on his professional achievements. "However," he went on, "If you *do* choose to mention my career, attached is my c-v," which ran to about fourteen pages! We spared the people in attendance the endless recitation of his very impressive career accomplishments.

My father met Shari for the first time in Washington, D.C., when he was receiving a Fifty-Year Lifetime Achievement award. Upon receiving it, he insisted that my crowd-shy mother join him on stage, and he put the award around her neck, giving her full credit for all that he had accomplished in his life. The pivotal moment, he said, was when he returned after World War II, and was considering abandoning his pursuit of a Ph.D in math, already in progress when he went off to fight. Apparently, Mom gave him an ultimatum: "Either you go back to school and finish your degree, or I'm leaving." She could be a tough lady.

Then when it came time to roll the casket out of the chapel, I followed it with my guitar, singing one of Dad's most frequently sung songs:

Show me the way to go home,
I'm tired and I want to go to bed
Well I had a little drink about an hour ago,
And it went right to my head.

Mom's end initially had a somewhat frantic element to it. She had begun the labored, difficult breathing that is common near the end of a person's life, and which is ordinarily controlled and relieved by morphine. Once again, we had morphine on hand provided by hospice, but I wound up calling hospice four times to ask for guidance, because one syringe of morphine hadn't seemed to help at all, nor did two—she was still desperately gasping for air—and then we added Ativan, then more morphine, and then finally hospice asked if I wanted a nurse to come over. "YES, PLEASE!"

The drugs finally took effect all at once, and Mom's breathing mercifully relaxed and slowed down…and slowed down further…and eventually it got to the point where after she exhaled, Shari and I would watch and wait, unclear whether she had died, and then suddenly she would take yet another long, deep inhale, and the process would repeat; she was taking about one breath per minute. This went on for a while, and then after one long, gentle exhale, the next inhale never came, and her twenty-year ordeal was finally at an end. It was around 11:30 on Friday night, November 29, 2019; the hospice nurse arrived forty minutes later, declaring her dead a day later on the Gregorian calendar.

According to the Hebrew calendar, Mom died on the second of Kislev, in the year 5780, and Dad on the tenth of Cheshvan, in the year 5777. It is traditional to light a 24-hour "Yuhrzeit" candle in memoriam on the anniversary of a loved one's death. To cover our bases, I agreed to light the candle according to the Hebrew date, and Harry settled on Veteran's Day each year.

All things considered, my parents' household was the most fun and happy solution to aging-in-place that I could have imagined, and I felt a deep sense of satisfaction and completion in my heart and soul that we had been able to take care of both my parents in the same way Dad had been taking care of Mom for so many years: keeping them in their own home, surrounded 24/7 by loving care and attention, and I was able to be physically present with them for their final six years, and for their final moments of life.

It was the very least I could do.

EPILOGUE

Dad has been gone for eight years now, and Mom for five. They were my whole world for most of my life, along with Shari for the last twenty-eight years. Yet I haven't truly experienced or expressed deep grief, and I don't believe I'm "pushing away" my feelings. As I said, I feel grateful and complete that Shari and I, with Harry consulting and frequently visiting, were able to be with them and do the things we did to keep them as comfortable as possible, and while doing so, reinforce that all-important factor that means the most in the end (and in the beginning and the middle): *connection*. I discovered that the experience of connection doesn't actually vanish with death, and that recognition took the edge off grief, for me.

Clichés only become clichés because they contain an element of truth, and I finally understood what I always viewed as a meaningless platitude uttered by clergy lacking imagination: "Your loved one lives on within you." Yes, of course I can no longer make my daily afternoon call to my father, but nevertheless, his and my mother's actual presence in my life, their essence and spirit inside my heart and mind, feels permanent to me. I still experience my parents right here, within my consciousness, where they have always lived for me. I have yet to experience losing my parents in any absolute and final sense.

When the great sage Ramana Maharshi was dying, his devotees were tearfully pleading with him not to leave them, and he responded,

"Don't be silly, where could I go?"

In a very real and tangible way, not in some mysterious or mystical sense, it feels to me as if everyone I have ever loved is still right here with me.

I don't find myself making the hour-long drive to visit their graves very often, because it also feels clear to me that their spirits are very definitely *not* located in the cemetery with their decomposing bodies buried beneath a headstone.

EPILOGUE

R.I.P Mom and Dad

Eliezer & Shari

AFTERWORD

The Day My Mother Lost Her Whistle

Harry J. Sobel, Ph.D.

My mother lost her whistle on August 10, 2008. She moved her lips but no sound emerged. I knew that Alzheimer's disease would slowly hide her soul, even destroy her conscious sense of self. We all knew that. I had watched her disappear over the previous few years, always recognizing the insidious grip that this implacable enemy held over our family, our shared memories. But somehow when my mother's whistle vanished with no fair warning, I felt a pain that had not as yet seeped into my own brain. My mother's whistle just disappeared. Gone.

You see, "the whistle" was not just any whistle. It was *our* whistle. It was the whistle my father invented in the 1950s in anticipation of one of us becoming lost in the crowds on the Jersey shore, next to the Belmar Beach boardwalk. We would wander off looking for just one more shell, or one more bottle cap, hoping for a few more minutes on the half-white summer sand. The whistle brought us home.

The whistle made it clear where one of us stood. No excuse could cloud our whereabouts. It was a life-affirming whistle that defined security. We knew that a parent was close at hand, but just far enough away to permit endless exploration. It was semi-freedom. The whistle? Well, it was a little family secret that was imprinted on each of us for the next half century. No cell phones, no email or texting, no iPhones. Just a simple C- Major whistle letting us know that all was okay.

It was 1956. Eisenhower. Ed Sullivan. Jackie Gleason. Cold War. Superman and Lois. Now it is 2013. Obama. Syria. Identity theft and climate catastrophes. Facebook, Twitter and LinkedIn. The whistle is gone from my mother's lips, leaving sadness illuminated just a bit more. I'll probably teach my children and my children's children all about the whistle, but perhaps I won't. We may need a new whistle, perhaps in D- Major, with a slight pianissimo trill. We certainly could use a smiling whistle to help us believe in safety amidst the onslaught of inexorable negative events these days. I knew 1956. And as former Senator Lloyd Bentsen might have said: "1956 was a friend of mine."

My mother has lost her whistle yet I hear its tone somewhere silently in the quiet heart that connects us. No disease will destroy that very safe space near the Jersey boardwalk, on a Sunday in August, 1956. It's a place I can go to with ease.

AFTERWORD

Eliezer (then "Elliot") & Harry, circa 1956

Harry & El about ten years ago.

ACKNOWLEDGMENTS

We were blessed to have had many wonderful and loving home healthcare aides pass through our home over the course of twelve years, including the very first, Dzulca B., who never missed a day of work or arrived a moment late, and always made herself available to step in to cover emergencies, sometimes enlisting the help of her beautiful daughter Selma and always-helpful husband, Jazminka.

Tanya H. was also with us since nearly the beginning, along with Natalie P., Sheka J., the late Daniela H., Maria W., Jessica W., Nefi N., and Bruce H. Finally, my mother's amazing and devoted live-in aide for her final years, the extraordinary Tamar A., who went on to become my father-in-law Marty's live-in aide once my mother passed, and who truly became a vital part of the extended Sobel-Cordon family.

My beloved Aunt Gerda, who called every single day, and visited my parents quite often, always with her daughter, my ever-loyal and kind-hearted cousin, Ellen Teitelbaum.

My father's former student and "BFF" in the last years of his life, Dr. Janice Shuhan, who visited him every day for years to take him out for walks and lunches, and participated in several middle-of-the-night rescue operations.

And finally, a very special thank you to my dear old pal, Marty Schrank, who generously offered the gift of his time and editorial expertise to this project.

Our family's deepest gratitude and appreciation to all of you.

www.ingramcontent.com/pod-product-compliance
Lightning Source LLC
Chambersburg PA
CBHW041503010526
44118CB00001B/3